Th...

Sta... ...g F... .. Spiritual
Warfare

The Bible Teacher's Guide

Gregory Brown

Publishing

Endorsements

"*The Bible Teacher's Guide* ... will help any teacher study and get a better background for his/her Bible lessons. In addition, it will give direction and scope to teaching of the Word of God. Praise God for this contemporary introduction to the Word of God."

—Dr. Elmer Towns
Co-founder of Liberty University
Former Dean, Liberty Baptist Theological Seminary

"Expositional, theological, and candidly practical! I highly recommend The Bible Teacher's Guide for anyone seeking to better understand or teach God's Word."

—Dr. Young–Gil Kim
Founding President, Handong Global University

"Helpful to both the layman and the serious student, The Bible Teacher's Guide, by Dr. Greg Brown, is outstanding!"

—Dr. Neal Weaver
President, Louisiana Baptist University

"Whether you are preparing a Bible study, a sermon, or simply wanting to dive deeper into a personal study of God's Word, these will be very helpful tools."

—Eddie Byun
Missions and Teaching Pastor, Venture Christian Church, Los Gatos, California
Author of Justice Awakening

"I am happy that Greg is making his insights into God's truth available to a wider audience through these books. They bear the hallmarks of good Bible teaching: the result of rigorous Bible study and thoroughgoing application to the lives of people."

—Ajith Fernando
Teaching Director, Youth for Christ
Author of A Call to Joy and Pain

"The content of the series is rich. My prayer is that God will use it to help the body of Christ grow strong."

—Dr. Min Chung
Senior Pastor, Covenant Fellowship Church, Urbana, Illinois
Adjunct Professor, Urbana Theological Seminary

"Knowing the right questions to ask and how to go about answering them is fundamental to learning in any subject matter. Greg demonstrates this convincingly."

—Dr. William Moulder
Professor of Biblical Studies, Trinity International University

"Pastor Greg is passionate about the Word of God, rigorous and thorough in his approach to the study of it... I am pleased to recommend The Bible Teacher's Guide to anyone who hungers for the living Word."

—Dr. JunMo Cho
Professor of Linguistics, Handong Global University
Contemporary Christian Music Recording Artist

"I can't imagine any student of Scripture not benefiting by this work."

—Steven J. Cole
Pastor, Flagstaff Christian Fellowship, Flagstaff, Arizona
Author of the Riches from the Word series

Contents

Preface...11

Introduction...13

Believers Stand Firm by Being Prepared...17

Believers Stand Firm by Knowing the Enemy...23

Believers Stand Firm by Fighting...33

Believers Stand Firm by Putting On the Belt of Truth...39

Believers Stand Firm by Putting On the Breastplate of Righteousness...47

Believers Stand Firm by Putting On the Footwear of Peace...55

Believers Stand Firm by Taking Up the Shield of Faith...63

Believers Stand Firm by Putting On the Helmet of Salvation...69

Believers Stand Firm by Taking Up the Sword of the Spirit...83

Believers Stand Firm by Praying in the Spirit...91

Conclusion...107

Appendix: Walking the Romans Road...109

Coming Soon...115

About the Author...117

Notes...119

Preface

And entrust what you heard me say in the presence of
many others as witnesses to faithful people
2 Timothy 2:2 (NET)

Paul's words to Timothy still apply to us today. We need to
raise up teachers who correctly handle and fearlessly teach
the Word of God. It is with this hope in mind that the Bible
Teacher's Guide (BTG) series has been created. This series
includes both expositional and topical studies, and is useful
for personal devotions and small groups, and for teachers
preparing to share God's Word.

In *The Armor of God: Standing Firm in Spiritual Warfare*, you
will learn how to stand against the enemy's attacks—
protected by the full armor of God. This Guide can be used
as a five- to eleven-week small-group curriculum, depending
how the leader chooses to divide the introduction and the ten
principles about standing firm. Every week, the members of
the group will read a chapter or more, answer the questions,
and come prepared to share in the gathering. Each
member's preparation for the small group will enrich the
discussion and the learning.

Introduction

Finally, be strengthened in the Lord and in the strength of his power. Clothe yourselves with the full armor of God so that you may be able to stand against the schemes of the devil. For our struggle is not against flesh and blood, but against the rulers, against the powers, against the world rulers of this darkness, against the spiritual forces of evil in the heavens. For this reason, take up the full armor of God so that you may be able to stand your ground on the evil day, and having done everything, to stand. Stand firm therefore, by fastening the belt of truth around your waist, by putting on the breastplate of righteousness, by fitting your feet with the preparation that comes from the good news of peace, and in all of this, by taking up the shield of faith with which you can extinguish all the flaming arrows of the evil one. And take *the helmet of salvation* and the sword of the Spirit, which is the word of God. With every prayer and petition, pray at all times in the Spirit, and to this end be alert, with all perseverance and requests for all the saints. Pray for me also, that I may be given the message when I begin to speak—that I may confidently make known the mystery of the gospel, for which I am an ambassador in chains. Pray that I may be able to speak boldly as I ought to speak.
Ephesians 6:10-20 (NET)

How can we stand firm in spiritual warfare?

In this text, Paul talks about the spiritual war every Christian is engaged in. When a person accepts Christ as Savior, he crosses over from the realm of darkness to the realm of light. He enters a spiritual war that includes demons and angels battling over the souls of men.

Sadly, many Christians live without any real awareness of this battle, and are therefore losing it. There are two wrong views of this battle: some see Satan and his demons in every cough, problem at work, or difficulty with their car. He gets far too much credit in many Christian circles. However, in other circles, Christians act as if Satan doesn't really exist. They know he is there, but they live without any true awareness of his activity in their lives.

We must recognize that Satan is real. He is an enemy of God and an enemy of the church. He tempts, traps, deceives, and kills, and nobody is exempt from his wrath. In light of this, Paul exhorts us to live the Spirit-filled life. In Ephesians 5:18, he calls believers to be filled with the Spirit, and then in the following verses, he looks at the results of the filling, including the Spirit-filled marriage, home, and workplace (v. 19-33, 6:1-9). A believer who is living a life of power—one that affects and changes people—will receive special attention from the evil one. He doesn't waste his best resources on those far away from God, but the closer a person gets to God and the more faithful he or she is, the more the enemy attacks.

It is not uncommon for me to talk to men and women who experience more problems the closer they get to God. The more they read their Bible, the more involved they get in church or ministry, the more problems they encounter. In fact, I remember one young man sharing the constant problems he experienced when faithfully reading his Bible,

14

and it made him not want to read it at all. This is exactly how our enemy works.

As seen with Satan's temptation of Adam and Eve in the Garden, he wants people to doubt God and to turn away from following him. There is no greater joy for the enemy than when a believer is angry at God or cursing him. That was his objective when attacking Job—he wanted Job to curse God (Job 1:11), and he wants us to do so as well.

In Ephesians 6, Paul talks about standing firm in spiritual warfare. The word "stand," or it can be translated "stand firm," (from *histēmi*), when used in a military sense, had the idea of holding a critical position while under attack."[1] He mentions our need to stand four times (v.11,13-14). Essentially, he says the wobbly Christian—the one not serious about God and trapped in sin—cannot stand in this war. He will be destroyed. Sadly, many fail to stand in this battle. MacArthur's comments are helpful in considering this reality:

> Countless men and women have faithfully taught Sunday school for years, led many people to Jesus Christ, pastored a church, led Bible studies, ministered to the sick, and done every sort of service in the Lord's name—only to one day give up, turn their backs on His work, and disappear into the world. The circumstances differ, but the underlying reason is always the same: they took God's armor off and thereby lost the courage, the power, and the desire to stand firm.[2]

How can we stand in this treacherous war and not miss our calling, be taken captive, or be destroyed? In this study, we'll consider ways to stand firm in spiritual warfare as seen in Ephesians 6:10-20.

Reflection

1. What is your experience with spiritual warfare?
2. Why is it important to stand against the schemes of the enemy?
3. What questions or thoughts do you have about this section?
4. In what ways can you pray in response? Take time to pray as the Lord leads.

Believers Stand Firm by Being Prepared

> Finally, be strengthened in the Lord and in the strength of his power. Clothe yourselves with the full armor of God...
> Ephesians 6:10-11 (NET)

In order to stand firm, believers must prepare for battle. This is true for any warfare—a soldier cannot be successful without preparation. Governments invest billions of dollars into training their soldiers both mentally and physically, and such commitment should be similar for Christians—no corners should be cut in becoming spiritually prepared. Many lose this battle simply because of failure to prepare.

Paul says to "be strengthened in the Lord and in the strength of his power. Clothe yourselves with the full armor of God." Essentially, Paul wants believers to understand that this battle cannot be won through human strength, but in God's strength alone. He talks about God's power throughout Ephesians. In Ephesians 1:18-21, he prays for the believers to know this power.

> – since the eyes of your heart have been enlightened so that you may know what is the hope of his calling, what is the wealth of his glorious inheritance in the saints, and what is the incomparable greatness of his power toward us who

believe, as displayed in the exercise of his immense strength. This power he exercised in Christ when he raised him from the dead and seated him at his right hand in the heavenly realms far above every rule and authority and power and dominion and every name that is named, not only in this age but also in the one to come.

This power raised Christ from the dead and put Satan and his demons under his feet (and therefore also under ours according to Ephesians 2:6). We must know that this power is in us. But also in Ephesians 3:16, Paul prays for the believers to be strengthened by it. He says, "I pray that according to the wealth of his glory he may grant you to be strengthened with power through his Spirit in the inner person." Finally, in Ephesians 5:18, he calls for us to be filled with the Spirit—meaning to be controlled and empowered by him.

A powerless Christianity is a vulnerable Christianity—in danger of being enslaved and destroyed by the enemy. This is what we see in most churches and in most Christians' lives—a powerless Christianity. We must constantly pray to know the power that is in us, to be strengthened by it, and to be continually filled with it. That is what Paul again calls for in Ephesians 6:10. "Be strong in the Lord and in his mighty power"—the same power that raised Christ from the dead and seated him in heavenly places over the enemy. We must put on the full armor of God so we can take our stand.

Since the verb "be strengthened" is passive present, the verse could also be rendered, "Strengthen yourselves in the Lord" or (NEB) "Find your strength in the Lord." It is the same construction as in 2 Timothy 2:1 where Paul exhorts

Timothy to "take strength from the grace of God which is ours in Christ Jesus" (NEB).[3]

In considering the armor of God, we must realize that throughout Scripture clothing often refers to attitudes and actions (cf. Col 3:12-14, Eph 4:24-25). The armor is God's clothing, as it essentially represents his character. Isaiah 59:17 says, "He wears his desire for justice like body armor, and his desire to deliver is like a helmet on his head. He puts on the garments of vengeance and wears zeal like a robe." Therefore, we prepare for battle by putting on God's power and God's character.

How can we be strong in the Lord (God's power) and put on his armor (God's character)?

1. We must recognize our weakness.

If we don't recognize our insufficiency for this battle, we won't put on God's strength and character. Therefore, to prepare us for a lifetime of battle, God often allows us to go through pain, trials, and failure first to show us our weakness. Paul said this in 2 Corinthians 12:9-10 about God's response to his request to take away the thorn in the flesh:

> But he said to me, "My grace is enough for you, for my power is made perfect in weakness." So then, I will boast most gladly about my weaknesses, so that the power of Christ may reside in me. Therefore I am content with weaknesses, with insults, with troubles, with persecutions and difficulties for the sake of Christ, for whenever I am weak, then I am strong.

Often trials are meant to reveal our weakness so we can see our need for more of God's power and character.

2. We must be dependent.

Again, Ephesians 6:10 can be translated, "Find your strength in the Lord." We need to depend on God to stand in this battle. Sadly, too many Christians are independent. You can see this in their lack of desire to read the Bible, pray, or fellowship with other believers. Why is this so common? It is because they are too independent. They believe that they can make it on their own.

However, the very opposite is true. We can do nothing without Christ. We are like sheep without a shepherd. We are like branches apart from the vine. John 15:5 says, "I am the vine; you are the branches. The one who remains in me – and I in him – bears much fruit, because apart from me you can accomplish nothing."

Are you abiding in Christ? Are you drawing near him daily? Or are you independent, and therefore losing this spiritual battle?

3. We must be disciplined.

The present tense of the verb "be strengthened" means that it is not a once and for all event—be strong—but a constant strengthening through God.[4] The implication of this is that we need discipline. If it were a one-time event we could stop working, but it is not. We need to continue to strengthen ourselves in the Lord.

Discipline is not only necessary to be empowered by God, but also to put on his character—his armor. First Timothy 4:7 says, "train yourself for godliness" or, as it can also be translated, "exercise yourself unto godliness." We need to practice spiritual disciplines—prayer, Bible reading, fellowship, serving, solitude, and giving—daily in order to become holy.

The Christian with poor spiritual discipline is like the soldier without discipline—unprepared and therefore vulnerable to attack.

4. We must be thorough.

Paul says to clothe ourselves with the "full" armor of God (Eph 6:11). Partial preparation will not do. If there are any chinks in our armor—which symbolizes our character—that is exactly where the enemy will attack. If we commonly struggle with unforgiveness, lust, anger, or lack of self-control, the enemy will attack in those areas. We must be thorough in this battle. In physical warfare, little compromises can get someone captured or killed, and it is the same in spiritual warfare. We must constantly repent of our sins and seek to get right with God. We must be thorough—putting on the full armor of God.

If we are going to stand in this battle, we must be prepared by knowing our weakness, depending on God, being disciplined, and being thorough.

Reflection

1. How is God calling you to seek his power and character in your life?
2. What are your spiritual disciplines like? How can you strengthen them?
3. What other questions or thoughts do you have about this section?
4. In what ways can you pray in response? Take time to pray as the Lord leads.

Believers Stand Firm by Knowing the Enemy

> Clothe yourselves with the full armor of God so that you may be able to stand against the schemes of the devil. For our struggle is not against flesh and blood, but against the rulers, against the powers, against the world rulers of this darkness, against the spiritual forces of evil in the heavens.
> Ephesians 6:11-12 (NET)

A crucial part of every army is the intelligence branch. Those who work in intel gather information about the enemy so the army can be equipped and prepared. In Ephesians 6:11-12, Paul gives intel about our enemy so we can be equipped to stand firm in this war.

Paul mentions the devil's schemes (v.11). The word "schemes" in the Greek is methodia, from which we get the English word "method." It carries the idea of craftiness, cunning, and deception. It was used of a "wild animal who cunningly stalked and then unexpectedly pounced on its prey. Satan's evil schemes are built around stealth and deception."[5]

Paul refers to awareness of the devil's schemes in 2 Corinthians 2:11: "so that we may not be exploited by Satan (for we are not ignorant of his schemes)." In order for believers to not be outwitted and to stand firm, they must know their enemy and his schemes.

What are some of the devil's schemes—his methods?

1. The devil uses accusation.

The name "devil" actually means "accuser." One of the devil's primary tactics against believers is to accuse and condemn. He accuses God to our ears—slandering his goodness and his faithfulness. Many people struggle with worship because they have accepted the enemy's accusations of God. As in Satan's attack on Eve, the enemy tempts us to doubt God's goodness so we will fall into sin.

But Satan also accuses us. He does this primarily through condemnation. After he successfully tempts us to sin, he then says, "Feel bad—feel really bad!" in order to further pull us away from God. Because of their stumbles, many Christians don't feel worthy to read the Bible, go to church, or serve. In contrast, the Holy Spirit convicts us of sin so we will draw near to God; he doesn't condemn us and push us away from God.

Finally, Satan accuses other people. He continually brings up the failures of others and seeks to draw us into anger, discord and unforgiveness. Many Christians have left the church because they listened to the devil's accusations.

One of his methods is accusation. He accuses God, us, and others.

2. The devil uses deception.

Very similar to accusation is the devil's tactic of deception. Jesus says the devil is a liar and the father of lies (John 8:44). He lied to Eve about God's Word and God's intentions. Since the devil oversees the world system, it is a system built on lies. He lies about what humanity is, what success is, what beauty is, and many other things. Satan lies in order to lead people away from God and his best for their lives.

He wants people to think they are an accident of evolution instead of the purposeful creation of God. He wants people to think that something is wrong with them—they are not pretty enough, smart enough, tall enough, tan enough, light enough, etc. We live in a world full of discouragement and depression because it is based on Satan's lies.

He also deceives people about the Word of God. The church is full of false teachings and cults because of the lies of the devil. First Timothy 4:1 calls these lies "demonic teachings." Second Corinthians 11:14-15 says, "And no wonder, for even Satan disguises himself as an angel of light. Therefore it is not surprising his servants also disguise themselves as servants of righteousness, whose end will correspond to their actions." He and his servants twist God's Word—creating false teachings or leading people to doubt the accuracy and inerrancy of the Word. He ultimately does this to lead people away from believing in Christ and God all together.

3. The devil uses persecution and fear of persecution.

Though the devil's favorite tactic is to use deception like a serpent, he often shows up as a lion to incite fear and to destroy. First Peter 5:8 says, "Be sober and alert. Your enemy the devil, like a roaring lion, is on the prowl looking for someone to devour."

In many nations around the world, he works to quiet believers or turn them away from God through fear and persecution. He roars so believers will be quiet about their faith instead of being the bold witnesses they are called to be. Christ describes the end times as a time of persecution, and a time when many will fall away from the faith because of it. In Matthew 24:9-10, he says:

> "Then they will hand you over to be persecuted and will kill you. You will be hated by all the nations because of my name. Then many will be led into sin, and they will betray one another and hate one another. And many false prophets will appear and deceive many."

4. The devil uses the world.

Since the devil is not omnipresent, he uses the world system to draw believers away from God. It is essentially a system without God—meant to lead and corrupt people. Satan uses this system to deceive and to conform people to his image. First John 5:19 says, "We know that we are from God, and the whole world lies in the power of the evil one."

We must be aware that Satan is over the fashion industry, the entertainment industry, education, government, and religion. When he offered Jesus the kingdoms of this world, it was a literal offer (Matt 4:8-9).

When Christians are aware of this reality, they keep themselves from befriending the world (James 4:4), loving the world (1 John 2:15), being spotted or polluted by it (James 1:27), and ultimately being conformed to it (Rom 12:2)—where they look just like the world (1 Cor 3:3).

5. The devil works through our flesh.

Our flesh is the unredeemed part of our bodies—it desires to sin and rebel against God. Though saved, we still carry this part of our nature, which came from Adam. When we give in to the flesh, we open the door for the enemy to work in our lives. Ephesians 4:26-27 talks about how anger gives the devil a foothold. But this is also true of lying, stealing, lust, unforgiveness, corrupt talk, and worldly thoughts. The devil works through our flesh.

We get a good picture of this in the account of Christ rebuking Satan while talking to Peter. Matthew 16:21-23 says:

> From that time on Jesus began to show his disciples that he must go to Jerusalem and suffer many things at the hands of the elders, chief priests, and experts in the law, and be killed, and on the third day be raised. So Peter took him aside and began to rebuke him: "God forbid, Lord! This must not happen to you!" But he turned and said to Peter, "Get behind me, Satan! You are a stumbling block to me, because you are not setting your mind on God's interests, but on man's."

What gave Satan the door into Peter's life? It was his secular, worldly thinking. He was mindful of the things of men and not the things of God. Man doesn't want to sacrifice—he wants prosperity, wealth, and health. Acceptance of death and sacrifice are not part of his old nature. Therefore, many people open doors to the enemy simply because their minds are still secular—their thinking has not been transformed through the Word of God (Rom 12:2).

6. The devil works through an army of demons.

Paul says this in Ephesians 6:12: "For our struggle is not against flesh and blood, but against the rulers, against the powers, against the world rulers of this darkness, against the spiritual forces of evil in the heavens."

Scripture teaches that demons are fallen angels. Revelation 12:4 says that at Satan's fall a third of the angels fell with him.

How many demons are there? We don't know. But we do know that Satan could spare up to 6,000 of them to focus on one person. In the story of the demoniac in Mark 5:9, the demons said their name was Legion. As a Roman legion consisted of up to 6,000 men,[6] the fallen angels appear to be innumerable. Satan has no shortage of allies, and all of them are seeking to destroy the people of God and the plans of God.

Paul doesn't teach us everything about demons, but there are many things that can be discerned from this passage.

What characteristics of demons can be discerned from Paul's teaching in Ephesians 6:12?

- Demons are supernatural.

Paul says we don't battle against flesh and blood. This means that demons are supernatural, and that our primary opponents are not evil people, but the power that works behind them. Wiersbe's comments are helpful here:

> The important point is that our battle is not against human beings. It is against spiritual powers. We are wasting our time fighting people when we ought to be fighting the devil who seeks to control people and make them oppose the work of God... The advice of the King of Syria to his soldiers can be applied to our spiritual battle: "Fight neither with small nor great, save only with the king" (1 Kings 22:31).[7]

- Demons are wicked.

Again, Paul says our struggle is against "the world rulers of this darkness, against the spiritual forces of evil in the heavens." Darkness symbolizes evil in the Bible. That is the demons' character—there is nothing good in them. They are the spiritual forces of evil. John Stott says this about demons:

> If we hope to overcome them, we shall need to bear in mind that they have no moral principles, no code of honour, no higher feelings. They recognize no Geneva Convention to restrict or partially civilize the weapons of their warfare. They are utterly unscrupulous, and ruthless in the pursuit of their malicious designs.[8]

- Demons are organized.

The demonic categories that Paul uses are not explained, but they seem to represent "differing degrees of authority, such as presidents, governors, mayors, and aldermen, on the human scale."[9]

"Word rulers" in the Greek is the word kosmokratoras or, with an anglicized rendering, "cosmocrats."[10] It can als be translated "cosmic powers" as in the ESV. This probably refers to demons that are set over nations or regions. In Daniel, we see powerful demons called "princes" over Persia and Greece (Daniel 10:20). The angel who spoke with Daniel was involved in a battle with two of these demons. In the same way, there are demons that rule like princes and generals over nations and cities—seeking to turn the people and the culture away from God. It is very interesting to consider that when Christ cast the demons out of the demoniac (Mark 5), they begged him not to send them out of the country. It seems that even the minions are territorial—focused on whatever territory or person they are assigned to.

Rulers, powers, and spiritual forces of evil also seem to reflect varying ranks. MacArthur says this about the "spiritual forces of evil":

> The spiritual forces of wickedness are possibly those demons who are involved in the most wretched and vile immoralities—such as extremely perverse sexual practices, the occult, Satan worship, and the like.[11]

What else can we discern about our enemy?

7. The devil wants to kill us.

Paul says our "struggle is not against flesh and blood." The word "struggle" was used of hand to hand combat—especially wrestling. However, wrestling in the ancient world was often a fight to the death.[12] This wrestling wasn't just for sport; it was deadly combat. The devil and his demons don't want to just tempt us and lead us into sin; they ultimately want to kill and destroy us. Jesus says this about Satan in John 10:10: "The thief comes only to steal and kill and destroy; I have come so that they may have life, and may have it abundantly."

When Satan leads people into ungodly language, secular thinking, selfishness, or compromise, though they may seem harmless at the time, he ultimately wants to lead them to their destruction. The devil is nobody to play with—he is a destroyer.

The only reason he has not killed us is that God is the ultimate sovereign. As in the story of Job, God sets boundaries on how far the enemy can go. If Satan cannot kill us, he is content to attack our bodies, our sleep, our joy, our peace, our testimonies, our callings, and our relationships—with the hope of destroying them. Our enemy is a murderer, and our only hope is our Shepherd—Jesus.

8.   The devil often attacks in an overwhelming manner.

Paul says for us to put on the full armor of God so that we may stand on the "evil day" (Eph 6:13). MacDonald says this about the evil day:

> The evil day probably refers to any time when the enemy comes against us like a flood. Satanic opposition seems to occur in waves, advancing and receding. Even after our Lord's temptation in the wilderness, the devil left Him for a season (Luke 4:13).[13]

Job experienced the "evil day" when the devil attacked his body, his family, his finances, and his friends for a season. This happens with many believers. Satan desires to make people give up, get angry at God, and turn away from him. A believer that is not being filled with the Spirit, who is not strong in the Lord, will fall prey to our enemy on this day.

Reflection

1.   What are some other characteristics of our enemy?

2. What is a healthy perspective for Christians to have regarding the devil and spiritual warfare? What is an unhealthy one?
3. What other questions or thoughts do you have about this section?
4. In what ways can you pray in response? Take time to pray as the Lord leads.

Believers Stand Firm by Fighting

> For this reason, take up the full armor of God so that you may be able to stand your ground on the evil day, and having done everything, to stand.
> Ephesians 6:13 (NET)

Paul writes of the need to stand firm four times in Ephesians 6; however, it must be remembered that this standing is not a passive, defensive stance. It is, in fact, active and offensive. Ephesians 6:17 and 19 tell us so.

> And take the helmet of salvation and the sword of the Spirit, which is the word of God... Pray for me also, that I may be given the message when I begin to speak – that I may confidently make known the mystery of the gospel

The sword was not primarily a defensive weapon, but an offensive one. As we share the Word of God with others, we are on the offensive. In fact, Paul prays for grace in sharing the gospel with others (v. 19).

It has been said that the best defense is a great offense. When the enemy is constantly being attacked, it is hard for him to mount an effective offense. Similarly, when Paul was going throughout the Gentile world spreading the gospel, he was fighting against the darkness. He was setting captives of Satan free by leading them to Christ. He was exposing the Roman world to light so that the darkness began to flee, and it must be the same for us.

We also see this in Christ's words about building his church in Matthew 16:18. He says, "And I tell you that you are Peter, and on this rock I will build my church, and the gates of Hades will not overpower it." The gates of Hades not prevailing is a picture of the church on the offensive. Believers are taking the battering ram of the gospel and breaking down the gates of Hades in communities, cities, and nations. This is a proper picture of God's battle plan for the church in this war.

How can believers fight this spiritual battle?

1. We must know what we are fighting for.

In a war, a soldier fights to protect his home, his family, his country, and his freedom. These things motivate him, and it must be the same for believers. If we don't know what we're fighting for, our spiritual lives often become dreary and lifeless.

What do believers fight for?

• Believers fight for the souls of the lost.

Jesus says this to Paul about his calling as an apostle in Acts 26:17-18:

> "I will rescue you from your own people and from the Gentiles, to whom I am sending you to open their eyes so that they turn from darkness to light and from the power of Satan to God, so that they may receive forgiveness of sins and a share among those who are sanctified by faith in me."

Similarly, Christians must recognize that they are on a rescue mission to save the lost from eternal darkness.

- Believers fight to please God and be rewarded by him.

Consider these verses:

Watch out, so that you do not lose the things we have worked for, but receive a full reward.
2 John 1:8

Instead I subdue my body and make it my slave, so that after preaching to others I myself will not be disqualified.
1 Corinthians 9:27

John calls Christians to be careful to not lose their reward, but rather to seek a full reward from God. Similarly, Paul was not afraid of losing his salvation, but he feared losing his reward and ultimately his usefulness. We fight to please God and to be rewarded by him. Believers with no desire to please God will not fight—they will remain spiritually lethargic.

- Believers fight to glorify God with their lives.

First Corinthians 10:31 says, "So whether you eat or drink, or whatever you do, do everything for the glory of God." Even our fighting in this war is for the glory of God. When Christ went into the temple and turned over tables, he was consumed with zeal for God's house (John 2:17), and with the glory of God. Similarly, we fight because we are consumed with the glory of God. A person not consumed with God's glory—God being exalted throughout the world—will not fight.

How else can believers fight this battle?

2. We must know that the war has already been won, and we must fight with Christ's authority.

Another important reality that every believer must understand when fighting this battle is that the war is already won. Therefore, we are not fighting to win, but because we've won. We see this taught in many texts, including the following:

> – since the eyes of your heart have been enlightened – so that you may know what is the hope of his calling, what is the wealth of his glorious inheritance in the saints, and what is the incomparable greatness of his power toward us who believe, as displayed in the exercise of his immense strength. This power he exercised in Christ when he raised him from the dead and seated him at his right hand in the heavenly realms far above every rule and authority and power and dominion and every name that is named, not only in this age but also in the one to come. And God put all things under Christ's feet, and he gave him to the church as head over all things. Now the church is his body, the fullness of him who fills all in all.
> Ephesians 1:18-22

> Disarming the rulers and authorities, he has made a public disgrace of them, triumphing over them by the cross.
> Colossians 2:15

This is important to understand so that we don't become discouraged and quit. Christ has already won this battle on the cross. Satan—the serpent—bit his heel, but Jesus crushed the serpent's head by his own death and resurrection (cf. Gen 3:15). He disarmed the evil powers and authorities, and was raised up in authority over them. Christians must remember this.

This is why when Paul encountered those possessed with demons, he cast them out in the "name of Jesus" (Acts 16:18). He declared Christ's authority over them. We must walk in this reality as well. Christ is seated in authority over the demonic powers; he disarmed them and has placed us in authority over them as well—because we are in Christ (Eph 2:6).

As Paul did, there may be times where you need to rebuke the devil in "the name of Jesus"—declaring Christ's authority. You may have to pray in authority over people stuck in spiritual depression (cf. 1 Sam 16:15), habitual sin (cf. Eph 4:26-27), or some type of demonic illness (cf. Lk 13:11). You may need to speak and stand on this reality in your own life, as you feel assaulted by the enemy emotionally, physically, and socially. Yes, the flesh and the world tempt and attack us, but we also must recognize this very real evil force—the devil and his demons—and the authority Christ has given us in his name (cf. Matt 28:18-19).

Reflection

1. Why is it important to be on the offensive in spiritual warfare?
2. What is your motivation to fight?

3. What other questions or thoughts do you have about this section?
4. In what ways can you pray in response? Take time to pray as the Lord leads.

Believers Stand Firm by Putting on the Belt of Truth

Stand firm therefore, by fastening the belt of truth...
Ephesians 6:14 (NET)

A Roman soldier wore a tunic under his armor, and a large leather belt "was used to gather his garments together as well as hold his sword."[14] The belt was the first part of the armor put on, and it held everything else together. It was crucial. Similarly, truth is a crucial component for every believer in this spiritual battle—without it believers are not prepared to stand and fight.

What does the belt of truth represent, how do we put it on, and how does it protect us from the enemy?

Commentators are divided on the exact meaning of the belt of truth. It could represent several things.

1. The belt of truth represents knowing the content of truth as revealed in Scripture.

Jesus said this in John 17:17: "Set them apart in the truth; your word is truth." The Word of God is truth, and it is through knowing and applying this truth that we are sanctified—daily made holy and righteous.

With that said, we can clearly discern Satan's attacks during this age. We can see it in the post-modern concept of relativism. We live in an age of no absolutes. It is the predominant philosophical thought taught in our education system today. Peter Singer, an ethics professor at Princeton and arguably the most influential modern philosopher, teaches that bestiality is not morally wrong (as long as it doesn't hurt the animal),[15] and neither is killing infants with disabilities.[16] Ironically, he teaches at the same seminary where Jonathan Edwards served as president!

Because of teachings like this, we are raising up a generation that is increasingly vulnerable to the devil. In their world-view, there are no absolute rights or wrongs. Therefore, sexual immorality, homosexuality, the murder of innocent infants, assisted suicide, and sometimes even gross injustices like pedophilia are not wrong. The only thing "wrong" is to declare the existence of absolute truth—for that you will be persecuted. We live in a system that is based on the lies of the devil, and if you don't know the truth, you will fall into the temptation of the day.

But Satan is not just attacking the culture with relativism and other fashionable lies, he is also attacking the church—the pillar and foundation of truth (1 Tim 3:15)—and specifically, the Word of God. With Eve in the Garden, he attacked God's Word. "Did God really say?" he asked. In the Parable of the Sower, the devil removed the seed on the wayside before it could produce any fruit (Matt 13:4). Our enemy always attacks the Word of God. In 1 Timothy 4:1, Paul talks about doctrines of demons that will lead some away from the faith. The enemy of our souls constantly assaults the church by twisting or denying Scripture—pulling many away from God. It is increasingly common for people to call themselves Christians and yet not believe that the Bible is true and without error, even though Scripture refers to itself as true, perfect, inspired, and enduring (cf. John 17:17, Ps 19:7, 2 Tim 3:16, 1 Peter 1:23). Jesus says man shall not live by bread alone but by "every word" that comes

40

from the mouth of God (Matt 4:4). He does not say "SOME" words, as many in the church today would teach, but "EVERY" word.

When believers accept the lie that not all Scripture is true, they are on a slippery slope. It is not too soon after that they throw out the virgin birth, the resurrection, the judgment, the miracles of Christ—soon leading them to discard the gospel and salvation altogether.

Saints, if you do not know the Word of God, you are not prepared to stand in this spiritual war. An ancient soldier couldn't even fight without cinching his belt—all his clothing would have hindered him. And neither can we fight without knowing the truth. Ephesians 4:11-14 talks about God giving the church pastors and teachers so his children would no longer be tossed to and fro by every wind of teaching, and by deceitful men. The enemy feasts on believers who don't know the Word of God, but at the same time, he is defeated by those who do know it. Consider John's description of spiritual young men in the church in 1 John 2:14. He says, "I have written to you, young people, that you are strong, and the word of God resides in you, and you have conquered the evil one." Spiritual young men overcome the devil because the Word of God is strong in them. Therefore, they are conquering their lusts, confronting false teachings, and helping set others free.

It is no wonder that many of the great warriors in church history have been men and women of the Word of God. It was said of Martin Luther that he essentially memorized the entire Bible in Latin. John Wesley memorized almost the entire Greek New Testament.[17] If we are going to win this battle, we must know the great doctrines of the Word of God.

In considering this, I would especially recommend that young believers systematically study the major doctrines of Scripture. It is harder to understand Scripture verse by verse in a short time, but easier to understand it systematically. Wayne Grudem's Systematic Theology, for example, addresses the doctrines of Christ, the Holy Spirit, salvation, end times, etc. Know what the Bible teaches on major doctrines so you won't be led astray by all the false teachings circulating in the church.

2. The belt of truth represents living a life of honesty and integrity.

The belt of truth does not represent just knowing the content of the truth, but also living out the truth practically in our daily lives. Ephesians 4:25-27 says:

> Therefore, having laid aside falsehood, each one of you speak the truth with his neighbor, for we are members of one another. Be angry and do not sin; do not let the sun go down on the cause of your anger. Do not give the devil an opportunity.

Practicing falsehood and hypocrisy opens the door to the devil in our lives—it gives him a foothold. Wiersbe says, "Once a lie gets into the life of a believer, everything begins to fall apart. For over a year, King David lied about his sin with Bathsheba, and nothing went right."[18] When David repented, he wrote this (Psalm 32:2-5):

> How blessed is the one whose wrongdoing the Lord does not punish, in whose spirit there is no deceit. When I refused to confess my sin, 9 my whole body wasted away, while I groaned in pain all day long. For day and night you tormented me; you tried to destroy me in the intense heat of summer. (Selah)

42

Then I confessed my sin; I no longer covered up my wrongdoing. I said, "I will confess my rebellious acts to the Lord." And then you forgave my sins. (Selah).

While David was living a hypocritical, dishonest life, he lost the blessing of God. He experienced sickness, depression, and physical weakness until he confessed his sins. As he said in Psalm 51:6, "Look, you desire integrity in the inner man; you want me to possess wisdom."

Lies and deception open the door to the devil; therefore, we must put off falsehood and practice transparency before God and others as we confess our sins (cf. 1 John 1:9, James 5:16). Satan likes to work in the shadows—he wants people to keep their sins in the dark instead of confessing them before God and man. It gives him a base from which to attack us. But the light of confession enables God to work in those dark places and set us free.

In what ways are you giving the enemy a foothold by practicing dishonesty? Is it through cheating on tests, lying on taxes, illegal downloading, or telling little fibs at work? In what ways are you practicing transparency—confession before God and man—in order to close the door on the devil?

In order to put on the belt of truth, we must practice honesty and get rid of all deception in our lives.

3. The belt of truth represents total commitment and zeal for Christ.

The metaphor of buckling or girding is often used in Scripture to describe the preparatory action of gathering one's flowing garments in order to work, run a race, or fight a battle.[19] Luke 12:35 says, "Let your loins be girded about, and your lights burning" (KJV). First Peter 1:13 says, "Wherefore gird up the loins of your mind" (KJV). These texts both refer metaphorically to the action of tightening one's belt so as not to hinder action.

Since buckling or girding is often used to describe preparation, some commentators think the belt of truth refers to serving the Lord wholeheartedly, with total commitment, as a soldier going into battle. John MacArthur says this:

> I believe that being girded ... with truth primarily has to do with the self–discipline of total commitment. It is the committed Christian, just as it is the committed soldier and the committed athlete, who is prepared. Winning in war and in sports is often said to be the direct result of desire that leads to careful preparation and maximum effort. It is the army or the team who wants most to win who is most likely to do so—even against great odds...To be content with mediocrity, lethargy, indifference, and half–heartedness is to fail to be armored with the belt of God's truth and to leave oneself exposed to Satan's schemes.[20]

Christ says that in order to follow him one must hate his father, mother, brothers, sisters, and even his own life (Lk 14:26). He requires total commitment—anything less is to not be his disciple. Everything that might hinder our walk with Christ must be removed. Uncommitted Christians are fodder for the enemy. He uses them to scatter people from Christ instead of gathering people to Christ (Matt 12:30).

Are you putting on the belt of truth? Are you daily seeking to know the full counsel of Scripture, or are you neglecting God's Word? Are you practicing truth, or are you practicing hypocrisy and deception? Are you fully committed to Christ, or are you half-hearted? We must put on the belt of truth to stand against Satan's attacks.

Reflection

1. Which aspect of the belt of truth stands out most to you and why?
2. How is the enemy attacking the truth throughout the world and the church today?
3. How is God challenging you to hide his truth in your heart to better stand against these attacks?
4. What other questions or thoughts do you have about this section?
5. In what ways can you pray in response? Take time to pray as the Lord leads.

Believers Stand Firm by Putting On the Breastplate of Righteousness

> Stand firm therefore ... by putting on the breastplate of righteousness,
> Ephesians 6:14 (NET)

The Roman soldier wore a tough, sleeveless piece of armor that covered the whole torso, front and back, from neck to waist. It was often made of leather, metal, or chains. The primary purpose of the armor was "to protect the heart, lungs, intestines, and other vital organs." [21]

What does the breastplate of righteousness represent, how do we put it on, and how does it protect us from the enemy?

As with the belt of truth, commentators are divided on what the breastplate of righteousness symbolizes. It could represent several things.

1.The breastplate of righteousness represents recognition of the imputed righteousness of Christ.

Second Corinthians 5:21 says, "God made the one who did not know sin to be sin for us, so that in him we would become the righteousness of God." Essentially, Christ took our sin at the cross and gave us his righteousness. This is the very reason we can come into the presence of God and worship him. When he sees us, he sees the righteousness of Christ. This is probably symbolized in Zechariah 3:1-7, where Joshua, the high priest, comes into God's presence wearing filthy clothes. Satan stands by Joshua's side to accuse him—and no doubt to declare him unfit to be in God's presence. However, God rebukes Satan and places clean clothes on Joshua, which probably represents imputing to him the righteousness of Christ. The Angel of the Lord says, "Remove his filthy clothes." Then he says to Joshua, "I have freely forgiven your iniquity and will dress you in fine clothing" (v.4).

It's the same for us. Our clothes—representing our character and works—are unclean to God. Even our righteousness is like filthy rags to him (Is 64:6). Even our best works are full of bad intentions—to be known, exalted, etc. However, God rebukes the devil and gives us clean clothes—the righteousness of Christ. This is the only reason we can stand in the presence of God.

Because the imputation of Christ's righteousness happens at salvation, many commentators say the breastplate of righteousness cannot represent Christ's work. How can we put it on if we are already wearing it positionally? However, we still need to recognize this work in order to stand against the accusations and condemnation of the devil.

Many believers, though they assent to salvation by grace, think it is their daily works that continue to justify them before God. When they fail to fully satisfy God's righteous requirements, the enemy quickly comes to condemn them and pull them away from God. By not recognizing Christ's work, they are agreeing with the devil. "You are right, Satan. I should not go to church; I should not read my Bible—that would be hypocritical." They agree with the devil's lies—opening the door for him into their hearts and minds.

However, we must not do that. We must continually declare the righteousness of Christ. "I am justified by grace—the unmerited favor of God—through Christ's righteousness. I can do nothing to justify myself before God. Every day I must throw myself upon God's gracious provisions. He provided the perfect Lamb that was slain so I could come into his presence."

Are you still depending on the perfection of the Lamb? If not, you will accept the lies and condemnation of the devil and allow him to pull you away from God. We must daily recognize the perfect righteousness of Christ to put on the breastplate of righteousness.

2.The breastplate of righteousness represents our practical righteousness.

But the breastplate is not just imputed righteousness; it is also practical righteousness. When we are living a righteous life, we are protected from Satan. However, when we fall into sin, we give Satan an open door to attack and defeat us. Again, Ephesians 4:26-27 indicates this, as it says, "Be angry and do not sin; do not let the sun go down on the cause of your anger. Do not give the devil an opportunity."

The Parable of the Unforgiving Servant in Matthew 18 also represents this truth. In the parable, a master forgave a servant a great debt, but the servant did not forgive his fellow servant a much lesser debt. Because of this, the master handed the servant over to torturers. Matthew 18:32-35 shares the master's judgment:

> "Then his lord called the first slave and said to him, 'Evil slave! I forgave you all that debt because you begged me! Should you not have shown mercy to

your fellow slave, just as I showed it to you?' And in anger his lord turned him over to the prison guards to torture him until he repaid all he owed. So also my heavenly Father will do to you, if each of you does not forgive your brother from your heart."

Obviously, the master reflects God and the servants reflect believers, but who are the torturers? No doubt, they are Satan and his demons. We see this throughout Scripture. When Saul was in unrepentant sin, who did God hand him over to? A tormenting spirit (1 Sam 16:14)! In the Corinthian church, when an unrepentant man was fornicating with his stepmother, who did Paul call for the church to hand him over to? Satan (1 Cor 5:5)! They would do this by putting him out of the church.

Sin opens the door for the devil into our lives. No doubt there are many Christians who, as a result of unrepentance, have psychological problems which are demonic in origin. There are Christians being tormented in their minds, bodies, emotions, work, and relationships because they have been handed over by God to the enemy until they repent.

Ephesians 2:2 says Satan works in those who are "disobedient"; however, a righteous life is a protection.

3.The breastplate of righteousness represents guarding our mind and emotions.

As mentioned, the Roman soldier's breastplate was used to protect the vital organs such as the heart and intestines. In the Hebrew mindset, the heart represented the mind and will. The bowels, or intestines, represented emotions and feelings (cf. Col 3:12, KJV).[22] Therefore, the breastplate probably represents guarding our mind and emotions. Solomon says, "Guard your heart with all vigilance, for from it are the sources of life" (Prov 4:23).

Satan realizes that if he can get our minds and emotions, that will affect our worship and our obedience to God. That's why he always works to implant wrong teachings and lies into our minds through books, music, TV, and conversation. Our minds affect our walk—how we live. But he also wants to get our emotions. Many Christians are emotionally all over the place, and part of that is a result of spiritual warfare. Satan stirs up people to criticize and condemn. He stirs up little romances with the opposite sex to distract us from focusing on God. He works to make believers worry and fret about the future so that they lose their joy. The enemy is cunning and keen. Therefore, we must guard our hearts above all else.

How can believers put on the breastplate of righteousness by guarding their hearts?

- Believers guard their hearts by recognizing wrong thoughts and emotions, taking them captive, and making them obedient to Christ.

    Second Corinthians 10:4-5 says,

    for the weapons of our warfare are not human weapons, but are made powerful by God for tearing down strongholds. We tear down arguments and every arrogant obstacle that is raised up against the knowledge of God, and we take every thought captive to make it obey Christ.

    Here we see that a major part of our fight is recognizing wrong thoughts and emotions, taking them captive, and making them obedient to Christ. For example,

51

Scripture teaches us to "not be anxious about anything" (Phil 4:6) and "in everything give thanks" (1 Thess 5:18). When we are struggling with anxiety or complaining, our hearts and minds are not being obedient to Christ. We need to confront wrong thoughts and emotions with the truth, confess them to God, and submit them to Christ.

Are you taking your thoughts and emotions captive? Scripture calls us to control our emotions. God says, "Rejoice in the Lord always. Again I say, rejoice!" (Phil 4:4). I must choose to obey even when I don't feel like it; I must bring my heart into submission to Christ.

- Believers guard their hearts by filling their minds with Scripture.

    Philippians 4:8-9 says this:

    Finally, brothers and sisters, whatever is true, whatever is worthy of respect, whatever is just, whatever is pure, whatever is lovely, whatever is commendable, if something is excellent or praiseworthy, think about these things. And what you learned and received and heard and saw in me, do these things. And the God of peace will be with you.

    If we fill our minds with truth and righteousness, then the devil will have less opportunity to tempt us. Every day we must fill our minds with truth by thinking on Scripture through our reading, worshiping, and even entertainment, if at all possible.

    Are you putting on the breastplate of righteousness? Are you recognizing Christ's imputed righteousness, living a life, and guarding your heart and emotions? Without these practices, you are opening the door to the devil.

Reflection

1. Which aspect of the breastplate of righteousness stands out most to you and why?
2. How do you recognize the difference between condemnation from the devil and conviction from the Holy Spirit?
3. What doors are still open in your life for the enemy? In what ways is God calling you to turn away from sin so you can put on the breastplate of righteousness?
4. In what ways does Satan commonly attack your mind and emotions? How do you take rogue thoughts and emotions captive and make them obedient to Christ?
5. What other questions or thoughts do you have about this section?
6. In what ways can you pray in response? Take time to pray as the Lord leads.

Believers Stand Firm by Putting On the Footwear of Peace

> By fitting your feet with the preparation that comes from the good news of peace
> Ephesians 6:15 (NET)

When Paul talks about "fitting your feet with the preparation that comes from the good news of peace," he is picturing the footwear of a Roman soldier. They typically wore a half-boot with the toes uncovered and spikes coming out of the soles. The boots allowed "the soldier to be ready to march, climb, fight, or do whatever else is necessary."[23] The spikes specifically helped when hiking or on slippery surfaces.

Without the right shoes, the soldier's feet were prone to blisters, cuts, and other problems which put him at a disadvantage in battle. The soldier's shoes were very important—without them, he wasn't ready to fight.

Similarly, there is appropriate footwear for believers to wear in spiritual battles. It is the readiness that comes from the gospel of peace. As with the other pieces of armor, commentators are not unanimous on what this represents. It could represent several things, as outlined below.

What does feet fitted with the readiness that comes from the gospel of peace represent?

1. The readiness that comes from the gospel of peace represents appropriating the believer's peace with God.

Romans 5:1 says, "Therefore, since we have been declared righteous by faith, we have peace with God through our Lord Jesus Christ."

This is important because the enemy always aims to separate believers from God. It is God who gives believers the strength to put on God's armor and the power to conquer the devil. Therefore, the enemy always seeks to separate Christians from the source of all that is good. Sometimes he uses lies to foster anger at God. He often begins by cultivating a wrong view of God. Believers start to believe that God doesn't love them or want what's best for them—that he just doesn't care. Satan creates a caricature of God—a God of wrath but not a God of love, a God of judgment but not a God of mercy. However, God is all of these.

We must put on the gospel of peace by remembering that Christ died to bridge the chasm between us and God. He paid the penalty for our sins and gave us his righteousness so that we could know God and come into his presence. Jesus says, "Now this is eternal life – that they know you, the only true God, and Jesus Christ, whom you sent" (John 17:3). Christ died so we could come near God and have an intimate relationship with him.

In fact, Christ always strove to correct the disciples' thinking about God. In Luke 11:13, he said, "If you then, although you are evil, know how to give good gifts to your children, how much more will the heavenly Father give the Holy Spirit to those who ask him!" Christ wanted the disciples to know that their Abba desired to give them the greatest gifts—and it's the same for us. Do you know that our God wants to bless us, and that if we're in Christ we're at peace with him?

What is your view of God? Is he unloving, removed, strict, and overbearing? If so, you need to put on the footwear of peace—by recognizing that Christ removed the barrier between God and us. A wrong image of God destroys our footing. We cannot fight if we don't see God as he is: our Father, our Abba, our friend, and our spouse.

Are you wearing the footwear of peace?

2. The readiness that comes from the gospel of peace represents having the peace of God.

Not only has God given each of us peace with himself, but we also have the peace of God. In John 14:27, Jesus says, "Peace I leave with you; my peace I give to you; I do not give it to you as the world does. Do not let your hearts be distressed or lacking in courage." The peace Christ had while asleep in the boat during the storm, the peace that enabled him to go to the cross, he has given to us. It is not God's will for us to live in anxiety, fear, and worry. Scripture says, "Do not be afraid," "Do not worry," and "Do not be anxious about anything" (Phil 4:6). Christ has given us the promise of his peace.

If you are worried, anxious, and fearful, you have the wrong footwear for this battle. Our enemy is a roaring lion seeking whom he may devour (1 Peter 5:8). The lion roars to incite fear in his prey. Some believers are fearful about their future; others are fearful about what others think or say. Others are afraid of failure. These fears undermine the footing of Christians—our readiness for battle comes from God's peace.

Therefore, God commands us to put on his peace. Colossians 3:15 says, "Let the peace of Christ be in control in your heart (for you were in fact called as one body to this peace), and be thankful." Paul also refers to the peace of Christ as clothing to be worn (cf. Col 3:12). As believers, we must let God's peace rule in our hearts—not fear of failure, losing our jobs, or rejection. Satan wants to lead us as slaves through fear, but God guides us as children through his peace (cf. Rom 8:15).

Do you have peace in your heart? Or are you tormented by fear?

First John 4:18 says, "There is no fear in love, but perfect love drives out fear, because fear has to do with punishment. The one who fears punishment has not been perfected in love." A good earthly father doesn't want his children worried about food, drink, and clothing. He doesn't want his children worried about their future. As much as he can control events, he does so for their good. It's the same with our heavenly Father—except that, unlike our earthly fathers, he is all-wise and all-powerful. He wants us to know that he loves us and that he works all things for our good (cf. Rom 8:28).

Are you wearing the footwear of peace, or are you wearing fear, anxiety, and torment?

How can we put on the peace of God instead of fear and anxiety?

Philippians 4:6-7 says,

Do not be anxious about anything. Instead, in every situation, through prayer and petition with thanksgiving, tell your requests to God. And the peace of God that surpasses all understanding will guard your hearts and minds in Christ Jesus.

- If we are going to have God's peace, we must reject anxiety and fear. They are not God's will for us, and they are sinful. They say, "God, you are not to be trusted," or "You are not in control."

- If we are going to have God's peace, we must learn to pray about everything. Prayer must become the atmosphere we live in. When we are not living in prayer (i.e. God's presence), the storms of life will constantly frighten and overwhelm us.

- If we are going to have God's peace, we must learn to give thanks in everything. When we complain, murmur, and criticize, we lose the peace of God.

3. The readiness that comes from the gospel of peace represents spreading the gospel.

The association of feet with the gospel is not uncommon in Scripture. Isaiah 52:7 says, "How delightful it is to see approaching over the mountains the feet of a messenger who announces peace, a messenger who brings good news, who announces deliverance, who says to Zion, "Your God reigns!" In Romans 10:15 (ESV), Paul says, "And how are they to preach unless they are sent? As it is written, 'How beautiful are the feet of those who preach the good news!'" One of our responsibilities in this war is to share the gospel with others. It is each person's assignment. Second Corinthians 5:18-20 says:

> And all these things are from God who reconciled us to himself through Christ, and who has given us the ministry of reconciliation. In other words, in Christ God was reconciling the world to himself, not

counting people's trespasses against them, and he has given us the message of reconciliation. Therefore we are ambassadors for Christ, as though God were making His plea through us. We plead with you on Christ's behalf, "Be reconciled to God!"

In hand to hand combat, if one side is only playing defense, he will eventually be defeated. He must also attack. Our battle as believers is not just defensive; it is, in fact, primarily offensive. We are called to advance the kingdom of God by spreading the gospel everywhere in the name of Jesus. If you are not doing so, you won't stand firm. The enemy's offensive will eventually swallow you up.

Are you spreading the gospel? Is that your purpose at school, work, and home, and with family and friends?

Our feet must always be ready with the gospel. First Peter 3:15-16 says, "But set Christ apart as Lord in your hearts and always be ready to give an answer to anyone who asks about the hope you possess. Yet do it with courtesy and respect."

I think this also shows us how Satan attacks. He wants to attack our zeal for the gospel. He wants to quiet us. If we have lost our zeal, then we no longer are wearing the footwear of peace.

4. The readiness that comes from the gospel of peace represents peace in our relationships with others.

This is one of the major themes of Ephesians. Paul teaches the mystery of the gospel that God makes the Jew and Gentile one in Christ. Consider Ephesians 2:12-14:

that you were at that time without the Messiah, alienated from the citizenship of Israel and strangers to the covenants of promise, having no hope and without God in the world. But now in Christ Jesus you who used to be far away have been brought near by the blood of Christ. For he is our peace, the one who made both groups into one and who destroyed the middle wall of partition, the hostility

Animosity between Jew and Gentile was a major issue for the early church. In Acts 6, the Jews neglected the Greek widows in the daily distribution while providing for the Hebrew widows. However, Paul said Christ is our peace—he has made us one.

Surely disunity is one of the major weapons the enemy uses against our churches. Sometimes he brings disunity through racism, as seen with the Jews and Gentiles in the early church. Sometimes he uses doctrine. What God means to equip and strengthen us, the enemy uses to bring division and discord. Most times, he just uses pride. Pride says, "My way is the only way, and it can't be done any other way." Churches divide over changing the color of the carpet, the music, the flow of worship services, and any other thing. The root of this is pride—"my way is the only way."

In attacking the church, Satan seeks to bring division. Remember, Paul says in Ephesians 4:26-27 not to let the sun go down while we are angry, and not to give the devil a foothold. Christ is our peace.

Are you living in peace with those around you? As much as depends on you, live at peace with all men (Rom 12:18).

Are you wearing the right footwear for our spiritual war? Are you recognizing our peace with God? He loves us and cares for us. Are you being filled with the peace of God in your circumstances? Are you sharing the gospel—always prepared to give a defense of the hope that is in you? Finally, are you living at peace with all men, as much as depends on you?

Reflection

1. In what ways does the enemy attack your readiness that comes from the gospel of peace?
2. In what ways have you experienced Satan's attacks through division in your relationships—friends, family, co-workers, and church members? How have those experiences affected you and your relationship with God?
3. How is God calling you to put on his footwear?
4. What other questions or thoughts do you have about this section?
5. In what ways can you pray in response? Take time to pray as the Lord leads.

Believers Stand Firm by Taking Up the Shield of Faith

> and in all of this, by taking up the shield of faith with which you can extinguish all the flaming arrows of the evil one.
>
> Ephesians 6:16 (NET)

The Greek word "thureos," translated "shield," referred to a large shield about two and half feet wide and four and a half feet high. It was designed to protect the entire body of a soldier. The shield was like a door—made of solid wood and covered with metal or leather. It was often dipped in water to extinguish the fiery arrows of the enemy.[24]

Armies often wrapped pieces of cloth around arrows, soaked them in pitch, set them on fire, and then shot them at the enemy. Upon contact an arrow would often "spatter burning bits for several feet, igniting anything flammable it touched."[25]

Our enemy also shoots flaming arrows at us. He shoots the arrows of criticism, fear, covetousness, anger, depression, doubt, lust, and every other temptation. In order to stand firm, we must take up the shield of faith.

What is the shield of faith and how can believers take it up?

1. The shield of faith refers to trust in God's person.

When Abram was struggling with fear, God said to him, "Fear not, Abram! I am your shield and the one who will reward you in great abundance" (Gen 15:1). Essentially, God said, "Trust me. I will protect you and reward you." Our protection is God himself and we must trust in him.

Putting on the shield of faith means running to God when life is difficult, when life is good, and when life is mundane. Believers without the shield of faith will run to everything else before God. When in a trial, they will run to coffee, to cigarettes, to relationships, to pity parties, etc. However, when we're wearing the shield of faith, we'll run to God. He is our shield—therefore we must trust him.

How can we learn to trust God more?

- Believers learn to trust God by knowing his character.

Proverbs 18:10 says, "The name of the Lord is like a strong tower; the righteous person runs to it and is set safely on high." In the ancient world, a person's name was not simply what he was called; it referred to his character. The writer of the proverb says that knowing God's character is a tremendous protection for us. The more we know God and who he is, the stronger we can stand in spiritual warfare.

At the same time, the less we know God and his character, the more prone we'll be to believe Satan's lies and stumble.

We must understand that God is perfect, all-knowing, all-present, and all-powerful. We must know that he loves us, cares for us, and wants the best for us. We must understand that he is sovereign and in control of all events—nothing happens apart from his watchful eye. If we don't understand this, we will be prone to anxiety, fear, and anger.

God works all things according to the purpose of his will (Eph 1:11).

- Believers learn to trust God by knowing his promises.

God has given us many promises to help us stand in spiritual warfare. Second Peter 1:3-4 says,

> I can pray this because his divine power has bestowed on us everything necessary for life and godliness through the rich knowledge of the one who called us by his own glory and excellence. Through these things he has bestowed on us his precious and most magnificent promises, so that by means of what was promised you may become partakers of the divine nature, after escaping the worldly corruption that is produced by evil desire.

When tempted to fear, we take hold of Philippians 4:6-7—if we pray and give thanks in everything, the peace of God will guard our hearts and minds. When we feel like giving up, we hold on to Isaiah 40:31— those who wait on the Lord shall renew their strength. When burnt out, we take courage in Proverbs 11:25—those who refresh others shall themselves be refreshed. When weak, we hold on to 2 Corinthians 12:9—God's power is made perfect in our weakness; therefore, we will boast in our infirmities and trials. When God seems distant, we hold on to James 4:8— if we draw near God, he will draw near us.

Are you taking up the shield of faith by holding on to God's promises? God has given us many promises to help us to stand in the day of evil.

- Believers learn to trust God by faithfully walking with him.

The longer we walk with God, the more we will trust him. As we watch God part our Red Seas, defeat our Goliaths, close the mouths of lions, and use the evil intentions and actions of others for good, it enables us to trust him more.

Are you spending time with God—being in his presence? The less you are with a person, the less you will trust them. In order to be ready for this battle, you must live in the presence of God—walking faithfully with him.

What else does the shield of faith refer to?

2. The shield of faith refers to dependence on the body of Christ.

In ancient times, the edges of this shield were "so constructed that an entire line of soldiers could interlock shields and march into the enemy like a solid wall. This suggests that we Christians are not in the battle alone."[26]

The enemy attacks from every direction, and we need one another to stand firm. Yes, doing so is a struggle since the church is not perfect, as God is. However, it is the means through which God chooses to impart his grace. He works through an imperfect body. If we don't avail ourselves of the body's resources, we leave ourselves more vulnerable to the devil's attacks.

For this reason, Satan works overtime to pull people away from the church by accusing and condemning it. Yes, the church is full of sinners; in fact, it is full of both weeds and wheat (cf. Matt 13:24-30). However, every army is full of people with flaws, but without trust in one another, no army can stand.

Therefore, in order to put on the shield of faith, we must depend upon the body of Christ—just like Roman soldiers depended on one another.

Are you depending on the body of Christ? Are you confessing your sins to one another and praying for one another (James 5:16)? Are you speaking the truth in love to one another (Eph 4:15)?

3. The shield of faith refers to living a life of faith—a life of serving God.

In ancient Roman armies, the people holding the thureos—the large shields—were always at the front of the army. They were the front line. When they lifted their shields, they protected those behind them. This also allowed the archers to shoot arrows while under their protection. Therefore, to put on the shield of faith means to live a life of faith—serving God.

It means stepping out of our comfort zone to serve in a ministry. It means using our gifts to serve the church. When we do so, we'll be criticized by others, and we'll be attacked emotionally, physically and spiritually by the enemy. But as we stand firm against these attacks with the shield of faith, we protect others and help them grow as they benefit from our faith.

To never get involved, use our spiritual gifts, or build others up means to not use the shield of faith. In fact, those not serving, not involved, often aren't the focus of the enemy. Why waste resources on somebody who's not fighting?

However, the more serious we get about God—the more we pursue God and serve others—the more Satan will attack us. In some ways, we should find encouragement from being attacked—this means we are a threat. And if we are not being attacked by the enemy, we should be alarmed. Maybe, we are not in the battle.

Are you daily taking up the shield of faith? Are you living a life of faith or a life of fear? Are you depending on the body of Christ, or are you independent? Are you on the front line or the sidelines? If we are going to stand firm, we must take up the shield of faith.

Reflection

1. What aspects of the shield of faith stand out most to you and why?
2. In what ways have you experienced more spiritual attacks while pursuing and serving God?
3. How is God calling you to take up his shield?
4. What other questions or thoughts do you have about this section?
5. In what ways can you pray in response? Take time to pray as the Lord leads.

Believers Stand Firm by Putting On the Helmet of Salvation

> And take the helmet of salvation and the sword of the Spirit, which is the word of God.
> Ephesians 6:17 (NET)

Here, Paul pictures the Roman soldier's helmet. James Boice's comments are helpful:

> The helmet had a band to protect the forehead and plates for the cheeks, and extended down in back to protect the neck. When the helmet was strapped in place, it exposed little besides the eyes, nose, and mouth. The metal helmets, due to their weight, were lined with sponge or felt. Virtually the only weapons which could penetrate a metal helmet were hammers or axes.[3]

In warfare, the enemy commonly attacked the head since the solder's mind controlled his decisions and reactions in a fight. To harm the head was to gain an advantage in combat. Our enemy, Satan, does the same.
What does the helmet of salvation represent?

1. The helmet of salvation represents assurance of salvation.

As with every other piece of armor, the helmet of salvation shows us how the enemy attacks. Here we see how he attacks the believer's assurance of salvation. Satan's use of assurance is actually two pronged. He seeks to assure professed believers who are not truly saved that they are, in fact, "safe," and he plants seeds of doubt in those who are truly saved, leading to discouragement and depression. Personally, I've noticed it is often the Christians who are walking faithfully with God that struggle the most with assurance. And those who are not walking faithfully with him are not very concerned about their salvation at all, even though they should be.

When true believers are constantly worried about their salvation, they are not much use to the kingdom of God. They typically don't evangelize or serve. They essentially stop growing because they are too concerned with themselves. This is why attacking the head is a common tactic of Satan—it makes a Christian unprofitable.

How can believers be assured of their salvation?

- Believers must recognize their need for assurance.

In many churches, pastors never teach on the need for assurance of salvation. It's almost a forgotten doctrine. However, this is unwise. Christ says this about the last days:

> On that day, many will say to me, 'Lord, Lord, didn't we prophesy in your name, and in your name cast out demons and do many powerful deeds?' Then I will declare to them, 'I never knew you. Go away from me, you lawbreakers!'
> Matthew 7:22-2

Many in the church profess Christ but are not saved. Jesus explains this in the Parable of the Weeds and Wheat (Matt 13:36-43). God plants wheat—true believers—and Satan plants weeds—false believers. Because of this reality, we must consider if we are truly saved.

Paul and Peter both taught the need for assurance. Second Corinthians 13:5 says this: "Put yourselves to the test to see if you are in the faith; examine yourselves! Or do you not recognize regarding yourselves that Jesus Christ is in you – unless, indeed, you fail the test!" Similarly, 2 Peter 1:10 says: "Therefore, brothers and sisters, make every effort to be sure of your calling and election. For by doing this you will never stumble into sin."

All believers must examine themselves to see if their salvation is real. This is not something to put off; we must eagerly pursue such assurance. The first step is to recognize our need for it in light of the fact that Scripture commands us to seek it.

- Believers must use the tests in Scripture to confirm their salvation.

Several portions of Scripture are written specifically for this purpose. The primary text is the book of 1 John. John says, "I have written these things to you who believe in the name of the Son of God so that you may know that you have eternal life" (1 John 5:13). In the book, he gives a series of tests so we can know that we have eternal life.

What are some of these tests?

1) The test of obedience.

First John 2:3-5 says,

Now by this we know that we have come to know God: if we keep his commandments. The one who says "I have come to know God" and yet does not keep his commandments is a liar, and the truth is not in such a person. But whoever obeys his word, truly in this person the love of God has been perfected. By this we know that we are in him.

Faithful obedience to God and his Word is a proof of true salvation. Christ says, "If you abide in my words, then you are truly my disciples" (John 8:31, ESV). If we don't love his Word and continually follow it, we have no reason to call ourselves Christians in the first place.

Are you abiding in his Word?

2) The test of love for Christians.

First John 3:14-15 says,

We know that we have crossed over from death to life because we love our fellow Christians. The one who does not love remains in death. Everyone who hates his fellow Christian is a murderer, and you know that no murderer has eternal life residing in him.

Similarly, Jesus says, "Everyone will know by this that you are my disciples – if you have love for one another" (John 13:35). If we are lacking a supernatural love for other believers, then we are not his disciples. At spiritual birth, the love of God is shed abroad in our hearts by the Holy Spirit (Romans 5:5).

I really struggle when I meet people who profess Christ but say they don't need to attend church. If they are true Christians, they will want to attend church. Why? Not just out of love for God, but also out of love for other believers. They will want to be with believers and use their gifts to build them up. They will want to pray with them and serve them. This is a natural fruit of love. If a person doesn't even want to be around the church, then they don't love the believers and surely they are not saved.

Do you love your brothers?

3) The test of doctrine.

First John 4:15 says, "If anyone confesses that Jesus is the Son of God, God resides in him and he in God." This is a proper acknowledgment of Christ's humanity and deity. (The name "Jesus" represents his humanity and "Son of God" represents his deity). This is what keeps many cult members out of heaven—they have bad Christology. To them, Christ was either not a man or not God. He was an angel or something else. In the above statement John was refuting the doctrine of the Gnostic cult, which was attacking the Ephesian church. It's also a problem in many cults today and for many professing "Christians." They believe Christ was a good man and a good religious teacher, but not the Son of God.

Do you pass the doctrinal test?

4) The test of not loving the World.

First John 2:15 says, "Do not love the world or the things in the world. If anyone loves the world, the love of the Father is not in him."

True believers are different from the world and the culture around them. Where the rich man was not willing to leave his riches to follow Christ (Matt 19:16-22), the true believer is willing to leave the praise, adoration and riches of this world for the kingdom of God (cf. Lk 14:26-27).

It is sobering to consider that the rich man was highly spiritual. We know he appeared righteous-because he kept the law; he also desired eternal life. Since we can't see the heart, we would have quickly taught him the Four Spiritual Laws, then had him say the Sinner's Prayer and join the church. Because he was an upright person and a successful businessman, he would soon have been an elder in most churches. However, he had never been born again. He was living for the riches of the world and not for God.

Many professed believers are kept out of the kingdom because they don't truly love God. They love him only for what they can get. They want the riches of this world—health and wealth—but they don't want a Lord and they don't want a cross. Sadly, this might be the majority of "Christians," especially because of the widespread influence of the prosperity gospel.

Are you willing to reject the world and the things of the world to follow Christ? Or—like the rich man—do you want both salvation and the things of this world?

5) The test of decreasing sin.

First John 3:6 and 9 says,

Everyone who resides in him does not sin; everyone who sins has neither seen him nor known him... Everyone who has been fathered by God does not practice sin, because God's seed resides in him, and thus he is not able to sin, because he has been fathered by God.

John says, "everyone who has been fathered by God does not practice sin." This was the professing Christians' problem in Matthew 7:21-23. Jesus said to them, "'I never knew you. Go away from me, you lawbreakers!'" They professed Christ, but lived a life of sin. True salvation always changes the lifestyle of believers (2 Cor 5:17). They still sin, but the direction and pattern of their lives will be different. They will practice living for God and yet stumble—sometimes repeatedly. However, the direction of their lives will have changed—they will be trying to serve and honor God.

Is there a pattern of decreasing sin in your life? Or do you profess Christ, but not live for him?

6) The test of persecution for righteousness.

First John 3:12-13 says,

> ...not like Cain who was of the evil one and brutally murdered his brother. And why did he murder him? Because his deeds were evil, but his brother's were righteous. Therefore do not be surprised, brothers and sisters, if the world hates you.

Because of their changed lives and values, believers will often be hated and persecuted by society. Jesus gives persecution as a test of salvation. In Matthew 5:10, he says, "Blessed are those who are persecuted for righteousness, for the kingdom of heaven belongs to them."

He essentially says that those who are persecuted for their faith are part of the kingdom of heaven. This doesn't necessarily mean that we will all be beaten, stoned, or jailed. Persecution often shows up in more subtle ways, like verbal abuse or being considered strange. First Peter 4:3-4 says,

For the time that has passed was sufficient for you to do what the non-Christians desire. You lived then in debauchery, evil desires, drunkenness, carousing, drinking bouts, and wanton idolatries. So they are astonished when you do not rush with them into the same flood of wickedness, and they vilify you.

Do others find you strange because you don't get drunk like everybody else? Do people find you strange because you have chosen to practice chastity until marriage? This is normal for a Christian. You will receive some type of persecution from the world.

7) The test of perseverance.

First John 2:19 says, "They went out from us, but they did not really belong to us, because if they had belonged to us, they would have remained with us. But they went out from us to demonstrate that all of them do not belong to us." In talking about those leaving the Ephesian church to join the Gnostic cult, John says that they left because they were never truly saved. This is the final truth that we will consider. Those who are truly born again will continue to walk with Christ and will never ultimately turn their backs on him (cf. Matt 24:13).
Similarly, Paul says this in Colossians 1:22-23:

but now he has reconciled you by his physical body through death to present you holy, without blemish, and blameless before him – if indeed you remain in the faith, established and firm, without shifting from the hope of the gospel that you heard. This gospel has also been preached in all creation under heaven, and I, Paul, have become its servant.

Our reconciliation to God is proved by a faith that endures and continues in the hope of the gospel.

Are you still following Christ? Is your faith enduring?

These are just a few of the tests. All the Beatitudes are essentially tests of salvation, and the book of James has many as well. James says, "Faith without works is dead" (2:26). If our faith doesn't change us, it won't change our eternal destiny either.

Are you continually examining yourself? Has God given you a love for the saints and for his Word? Do you believe that Jesus is the perfect God-man?

Again, this challenge to test our salvation has almost been lost in the church. Therefore, we are amassing professing believers who are not really saved. And many who are saved don't know how to put on the helmet of salvation—referring to assurance—which makes them an easy target for the accusations of the devil.

Paul often teaches assurance side by side with the need to respond to the gospel. In Acts 26:20 he says, "but I declared to those in Damascus first, and then to those in Jerusalem and in all Judea, and to the Gentiles, that they should repent and turn to God, performing deeds consistent with repentance." Essentially, we prove our salvation by growing and producing the fruit of righteousness (cf. 2 Peter 1:10, 5-9).

It should be noted that salvation is eternal. Eternal security is an objective reality based on what Christ has done for us. He gives us eternal life and he keeps us (cf. John 6:37-39, John 10:27-30, Rom 8:38-39). Those who are truly saved will never lose their salvation. They will persevere in following Christ to the end.

However, assurance is not eternal. It is a subjective experience given by the Holy Spirit, and it can be temporary. Romans 8:15-16 says,

> For you did not receive the spirit of slavery leading again to fear, but you received the Spirit of adoption, by whom we cry, "Abba, Father." The Spirit himself bears witness to our spirit that we are God's children.

The Holy Spirit assures our hearts primarily by changing us into the Father's image—making us holy. Therefore, when believers are faithfully walking with God, they can clearly discern the Holy Spirit's assurance that they are children of God. But when believers are living in sin, they commonly start to lose that assurance.

Do you have assurance? Do you have on the helmet of salvation? Satan wants to steal the joy of your salvation. He wants to steal your calling and the good works God has called you to. If you don't know you're saved, then your head is vulnerable and you're not prepared to fight.

What else could the helmet of salvation represent?

2. The helmet of salvation represents anticipation of our future salvation.

First Thessalonians 5:8 says, "But since we are of the day, we must stay sober by putting on the breastplate of faith and love and as a helmet our hope for salvation." Paul calls the helmet the hope of salvation. James Boice's comments are helpful here:

> If that is what he is thinking of here, then he is looking to our destiny rather than our present state.

He is saying that our anticipation of that end will protect our heads in the heat (and often confusion) of the battle.[27]

Therefore, if we have lost the hope of our future salvation, we will not be able to stand in this spiritual battle. The luxuries of the world will draw us into idolatry and spiritual lethargy; the trials and persecutions in this world will draw our hearts away from God and our heavenly home. However, when believers hope in their salvation, that hope keeps them from living for the world and/or fearing persecution by the world.

Consider what Paul says in 2 Corinthians 4:16-18:

Therefore we do not despair, but even if our physical body is wearing away, our inner person is being renewed day by day. For our momentary, light suffering is producing for us an eternal weight of glory far beyond all comparison because we are not looking at what can be seen but at what cannot be seen. For what can be seen is temporary, but what cannot be seen is eternal.

Paul says he and the other apostles did not lose heart during their trials because their eyes were fixed on eternity. His trials seemed like light afflictions because he was focused on the glory of heaven. This focus kept him from becoming unraveled when going through temporary trials. He was wearing the helmet of salvation. In Philippians 1:21, Paul says, "For to me, living is Christ and dying is gain." He was ready to die a martyr for Christ because of his hope in salvation.

And surely this is true of many great missionaries who go into foreign territories and wage war against the powers and principalities for the souls of men. They do not hold their lives or comfort dear because their hope is eternal. Their eyes are fixed on the unseen and not on the seen. And this must be true for us as well.

Here we can discern one of Satan's most effective modes of attack. He attacks our heads by drawing our attention away from the eternal to the temporary. If our hope is on earth and earthly things—jobs, promotions, wealth, health, and the applause of men—we will be ineffective soldiers in this spiritual war. We will be unstable—up and down with the events of life. The enemy will continually attack our heads because they are unprotected—they are focused on the world instead of eternity.

Is death really gain for you, or is it the loss of all you live for? Can you rejoice while going through a trial, not getting promoted, or going through criticism—because your hope is on heavenly things and not on earthly things? If so, you are ready for war—you are ready to stand firm in this spiritual battle.

Reflection

1. What is your belief about eternal security? Can believers lose their salvation, or is it eternally kept by Christ? Briefly support your view.
2. How can believers gain assurance of their salvation, and why is it important?
3. If the helmet of salvation refers to our hope of salvation, how can we keep our eyes on the eternal instead of the earthly?
4. What other questions or thoughts do you have about this section?

5. In what ways can you pray in response? Take time to pray as the Lord leads.

Believers Stand Firm by Taking Up the Sword of the Spirit

> And take the helmet of salvation and the sword of the Spirit, which is the word of God.
> Ephesians 6:17 (NET)

The sword Paul refers to is not the broadsword (rhomphaia) but the dagger (machaira), which varied in length from six to eighteen inches. It was the common sword used by Roman soldiers in hand-to-hand combat, and was carried in a sheath attached to the belt.[28]

A skillful soldier used it to deflect the blows of his enemy, and the Word of God must be used in this fashion. We get a picture of this when Satan attacked Christ in the wilderness (Matt 4). To each of Satan's temptations, Christ responded with Scripture. Therefore, the Christian who does not know the Word of God well will have problems defending against the attacks of the devil.

What's interesting about Paul's description of the sword as the "word" of God is the Greek term used. John MacArthur says:

> The term Paul uses here for word is not logos, which refers to general statements or messages, but is rhēma, which refers to individual words or particular statements. The apostle is therefore not talking here about general knowledge of Scripture, but is

emphasizing again the precision that comes by knowledge and understanding of specific truths.[29]

James Boice adds:

While logos embraces nearly everything, rhēma has a slighter weight. It really means "a saying," in this case, a particular, specific portion of God's written revelation. John 3:16 is a rhēma. Romans 3:23 is a rhēma, and so on for all the other specific portions of the written "Word of God." It is important to see this, as I said, because according to Paul's teaching we are to overcome Satan by the particular words or portions of Scripture.[30]

This emphasizes the extreme power of each Scripture verse. Christ said that man shall not live by bread alone but by "EVERY" word that comes from the mouth of God (Matt 4:4). Scripture is God-inspired and powerful. It can translate a person from darkness to light and defeat the attacks of the devil. Therefore, we must know and love God's Word.

However, even though most Christians would say they believe this, in practice they deny it. Though they know Scripture equips the man of God for all righteousness and that each saying is powerful (cf. 2 Tim 3:16-17), they largely neglect it. Sadly, this is also seen in most preaching today. Instead of messages that drive the sword home, setting people free from sin and sharpening their consciences, most sermons are a chain of illustrations to support the pastor's thoughts, which may or may not come from Scripture.

For some preachers, this happens because of laziness. It takes hard work to really preach God's Word. But for many, it probably happens simply because they don't really believe how powerful each Word from God is. Each rhema—each verse of Scripture—is a surgical scalpel—needed to save and heal lives. We cannot fend off Satan with stories and illustrations, no matter how much people enjoy them. They need the Word of God.

Both in the pulpit and in the pew, people profess to believe in the power and necessity of the Word of God, yet they deny it by their actions.

Moses tells the Jews to talk about the Word of God at home, when walking along the road, when lying down, and when getting up (Deut 6:7). At that time, the Jews had only a few books of the Bible to talk about, but we have the whole written counsel of God. However, we probably talk about it much less than they did.

How do we take up the sword of the Spirit?

The word "take" is a command. If we are going to fight this spiritual battle, we must take the sword of the Spirit—the Word of God.

1. We take up the sword of the Spirit by reading Scripture.

Most Christians have never completely read the Bible. By reading 3.25 chapters a day, or slightly over twelve minutes a day, one can complete the Bible in a year. Or, if a person reads only thirteen chapters a day, they can complete the Bible in three months. Isn't it do-able to read six or seven chapters in the morning and six or seven at night to complete the Bible in three months?

Are you taking up your sword by reading Scripture daily?

2. We take up the sword of the Spirit by memorizing Scripture.

85

Again, the "word" of God Paul refers to in 2 Tim 3:17 is specific sayings—not the whole of Scripture. Christ defeated the devil with specific Scriptures committed to memory. Similarly, Psalm 119:11 says, "In my heart I store up your words, so I might not sin against you."

Each verse that we memorize is a dagger to help us in spiritual warfare. How many daggers do you have memorized? If we memorize one verse a week that equals fifty-two verses a year.

3. We take up the sword of the Spirit by meditating on Scripture.

Psalm 1:2 talks about the blessing on the man who meditates on the law of God day and night. The word "meditate" in the Hebrew was used of a cow chewing its cud. A cow has a chambered stomach with four compartments. It chews and swallows its food, then regurgitates it and repeats the process. This usage of the word "meditate" also has the connotation of muttering under the breath. The Hebrew word used can be translated "ponder" or "declare."[31] It means to speak God's Word over and over again, both audibly and inaudibly.

God blesses the person who thinks and speaks about the Word of God all day. This person is taking up the sword of the Spirit.

Are you meditating on Scripture all day long—pondering it and talking about it?

4. We take up the sword of the Spirit by studying Scripture.

Second Timothy 2:15 (KJV) says, "Study to shew thyself approved unto God, a workman that needeth not to be ashamed, rightly dividing the word of truth." "Study," which can also be translated "Be diligent" or "Do your best," obviously overlaps with reading, memorizing and meditating. *How can we practice studying Scripture?*

- We study by taking notes during sermons, Bible studies, and our devotions in order to help commit the truths to memory.

- We study by comparing portions of Scripture with other portions in order to better understand the meaning and application.

- We study by using tools to increase our understanding, such as a study Bible, concordance, commentary, or theological dictionary (cf. Eph 4:11-13).

- We study by writing the truths in a systematic manner to organize our thoughts.

- We study by teaching the truths we're learning to others, which is the most effective way to internalize something.

One of the problems in the church today is that people don't want to study the Bible. They are "sluggish in hearing," and have to be retaught the same truths over and over. Hebrews 5:11-12 says this:

On this topic we have much to say and it is difficult to explain, since you have become sluggish in hearing. For though you should in fact be teachers by this time, you need someone to teach you the beginning elements of God's utterances. You have gone back to needing milk, not solid food.

I think it is especially important for parents to teach their children how to study the Bible and not just listen—otherwise they will continue to lose what they learn. Again, 2 Timothy 2:15 says those who study—those who do their best—will be approved by God. Those who do not study don't really care about the truths they hear, and will therefore forget them. These people will not be approved by God.

Since our churches are filled with people who don't study (or care to study), most pastors can't teach the depths of God's Word. The writer of Hebrews says he wants to teach them more, but he can't because the congregation is "sluggish in hearing." What's happened in our day is that the church no longer teaches doctrine, but has handed that sacred task over to Bible colleges and seminaries. Most church services are filled with the milk of God's Word instead of the meat.

Doctrine needs to be restored to God's church, but the church also needs to be prepared to receive it. It's inspiring to read the sermons of Martin Luther, John Calvin, Jonathan Edwards, and Martyn Lloyd-Jones—the content is amazingly deep. For example, Martyn Lloyd-Jones preached 232 sermons on the book of Ephesians over an 8-year period (1954-1962).[32] However, the only way people can receive such content is by studying it.

If you're going to stand against Satan's attacks, you must take up the Sword of the Spirit—the Word of God—by reading, meditating on, memorizing, and studying it.

Reflection

1. What is your Bible study routine like? Rate it 1 to 10 and explain why.
2. What are some useful disciplines that help with studying the Bible?
3. What other questions or thoughts do you have about this section?
4. In what ways can you pray in response? Take time to pray as the Lord leads.

Believers Stand Firm by Praying in the Spirit

> With every prayer and petition, pray at all times in the Spirit, and to this end be alert, with all perseverance and requests for all the saints. Pray for me also, that I may be given the message when I begin to speak – that I may confidently make known the mystery of the gospel, for which I am an ambassador in chains. Pray that I may be able to speak boldly as I ought to speak.
> Ephesians 6:18-20 (NET)

Paul talks about spiritual warfare in this final section of Ephesians. In Ephesians 6:10-17, he details the believer's need to be filled with the power of God, and also to put on the full armor of God in order to stand against the attacks of the devil. The armor of God represents attitudes and actions that believers must practice to win on the spiritual battlefield. It includes the belt of truth, the breastplate of righteousness, the footwear of peace, the shield of faith, the helmet of salvation, and the sword of the Spirit. No Christian soldier can win without them; however, even these are not enough. We must pray in the Spirit.

We can see Paul's emphasis on the importance of prayer in two ways. First, he writes more about prayer than about any other piece of armor. He uses three verses to teach on prayer in the Spirit. Also, praying in the Spirit is the seventh piece of armor. In Scripture, seven is the number of completion. This means that one can be suited up with every other piece of armor and yet still lose the battle. Praying in the Spirit is a necessity.

Prayer is the energy and atmosphere in which we wage war. Believers must live in prayer at all times in order to win this spiritual battle. It is how we are strengthened in the power of God, and it is how we put on the full armor (cf. Eph 6:10-11).

I think we can discern the importance of prayer by considering the battle between Israel and Amalek in Exodus 17. Joshua led Israel's army into battle, but they only won while Moses prayed. When Moses became tired of lifting his hands in prayer, Israel began to lose. And this is true for us as well. We can read the Word, preach, evangelize, and live a moral life, but if we are not praying, we will be defeated.

Similarly, when Peter was going to be tempted by Satan right before Christ's death, the Lord told him that he needed to pray in order not to fall into temptation (Matt 26:41). Peter fell asleep and therefore did not stand in the evil day. We are often like this as well. We sleep when we should be praying. We fight when we should be waiting on the Lord. Prayer is essential. "Edward Payson said: 'Prayer is the first thing, the second thing, the third thing necessary to minister. Pray, therefore, my dear brother, pray, pray, pray.'"[33]

Again, Paul doesn't call us to just any type of prayer, but specifically prayer in the Spirit. What is prayer in the Spirit? Praying in the Spirit does not refer to speaking in tongues or any other charismatic experience. It simply means to pray according to God's Word and according to his promptings. Jude also commands us to do this in Jude 1:20. He says, "But you, dear friends, by building yourselves up in your most holy faith, by praying in the Holy Spirit."

As we consider praying in the Spirit, we must ask, "What are the characteristics of this type of prayer?" It is important to know the answer so we can tell if we are indeed praying in the Spirit.

In this study, we will consider the characteristics of praying in the Spirit as seen in Ephesians 6:18-20. We will give more attention to this piece of armor than the others, even as Paul does.

What are some aspects of prayer in the Spirit?

Prayer in the Spirit Is Constant

> With every prayer and petition, pray at all times in the Spirit ...
> Ephesians 6:18

Paul says that in this spiritual war, we must pray at "all times"—we must live in constant prayer. This is how the early church prayed right before Pentecost. Acts 1:14 says, "All these continued together in prayer with one mind, together with the women, along with Mary the mother of Jesus, and his brothers." The 120 remaining followers of Christ met daily and devoted themselves to constant prayer. This was necessary for God to use them to turn the world upside down, as seen throughout the book of Acts. Similarly, 1 Thessalonians 5:17 says, "constantly pray," which can also be translated, "Pray without ceasing."

How do we pray without ceasing—on all occasions?

Does "pray without ceasing" mean we need to have a running dialogue with the Lord throughout the day? Not necessarily. Steve Cole shares helpful insight about the phrase "without ceasing":

The Greek word translated without ceasing was used of a hacking cough and of repeated military assaults. Someone with a hacking cough does not cough every second, but rather he coughs repeatedly and often. He never goes very long without coughing. In the case of repeated military assaults, the army makes an assault then regroups and attacks again and again until it conquers the city. In the same way, we should pray often and repeatedly until we gain the thing for which we are praying.[34]

"Prayer is not so much the articulation of words as the posture of the heart."[35] John MacArthur adds:

To pray at all times is to live in continual God consciousness, where everything we see and experience becomes a kind of prayer, lived in deep awareness of and surrender to our heavenly Father. To obey this exhortation means that, when we are tempted, we hold the temptation before God and ask for His help. When we experience something good and beautiful, we immediately thank the Lord for it. When we see evil around us, we pray that God will make it right and be willing to be used of Him to that end. When we meet someone who does not know Christ, we pray for God to draw that person to Himself and to use us to be a faithful witness. When we encounter trouble, we turn to God as our Deliverer. In other words, our life becomes a continually ascending prayer, a perpetual communing with our heavenly Father.[36]

If we are going to win this spiritual battle, we must learn how to pray without ceasing. We must return to it throughout the day like a hacking cough, and like an army launching continual military assaults. We must train ourselves to live in God's presence—bringing every thought and concern before the Lord. This is necessary in our spiritual battle.

Are you practicing prayer on all occasions?

Prayer in the Spirit Is Varied

> With every prayer and petition, pray at all times in the Spirit ...
> Ephesians 6:18

Praying in the Spirit includes "every prayer and petition." "Prayer" is a general term for various types of prayer, and "petition" is a specific type of prayer. Sadly, most Christians use only one type of prayer—petitions (or requests). They only come to God to ask for things. However, when the Spirit of God leads our prayer, he leads us into various types of prayer such as thanksgiving and worship, intercession, confession, lament, and corporate prayer, among others. All these types of prayer have the power to defeat the enemy.

When Israel shouted in worship while standing outside Jericho, the walls fell down (Joshua 6). When Jehoshaphat and the army worshiped while being attacked, God defeated the enemy (2 Chr 20). Many times when we are tempted to complain and worry, the Spirit of God calls us to praise in faith and God defeats our enemies.

In addition, the practice of corporate prayer carries much power. Consider what Jesus says in Matthew 18:19-20, "Again, I tell you the truth, if two of you on earth agree about whatever you ask, my Father in heaven will do it for you. For where two or three are assembled in my name, I am there among them." Jesus teaches that corporate prayer carries tremendous power, and that when it occurs, God is with us in a special way. Similarly, James 5:16 says, "So confess your sins to one another and pray for one another so that you may be healed. The prayer of a righteous person has great effectiveness."

Some Christians never access this type of prayer because they never share their burdens with others or carry others' burdens; therefore, they lack power. There are some things God does only when his people pray together.

When the Spirit of God is leading prayer, he leads us to pray in a variety of ways. A good picture of this is seen in the Lord's Prayer, which Christ gave as a pattern. Consider the following types of prayer:

- "Our Father in heaven, may your name be honored" (Matt. 6:9) calls us into worship, as we pray for others to worship as well.
- "May your kingdom come, may your will be done on earth as it is in heaven" (Matt. 6:10) calls us to pray for missions, evangelism, and discipleship.
- "Give us today our daily bread" (Matt. 6:11), calls us to pray for our personal needs and those of others.
- "And forgive us our debts, as we ourselves have forgiven our debtors" (Matt. 6:12), calls us to confess our sins and those of others.
- "And do not lead us into temptation, but deliver us from the evil one." (Matt. 6:13) calls us to pray for spiritual protection from temptation and the devil.

It is a good practice to pray often through the Lord's Prayer.

Prayer in the Spirit Is Watchful

> With every prayer and petition, pray at all times in the Spirit, and to this end be alert, with all perseverance and requests for all the saints. Ephesians 6:18

Another aspect of praying in the Spirit is being watchful. Paul says, "and to this end be alert." This is military terminology. It pictures a soldier on duty watching for signs of either infiltration by the enemy or advancement by his fellow soldiers. As Peter says in 1 Peter 5:8, "Be sober and alert. Your enemy the devil, like a roaring lion, is on the prowl looking for someone to devour."

Our enemy is like a prowling lion; therefore, we must always be alert. Christ warned his disciples right before he went to the cross in Matthew 26:41, "Stay awake and pray that you will not fall into temptation. The spirit is willing, but the flesh is weak." He called for the disciples to pray so they wouldn't fall into temptation. He called them to be aware of what the enemy was doing around them.

How can Christian soldiers practice being alert in their prayer lives?

1. Christian soldiers practice being alert both by using their natural senses (like their eyes and ears), and by listening to the Spirit's promptings in order to discern the work of the evil one.

Is someone being unfaithful to the church or small group? Let us pray for God to draw them back. Is there discord in the body of Christ? Let us pray for unity. Is someone discouraged? Let us pray for joy.

What difficulties or attacks of the enemy are happening around you? How is God calling you to intercede?

2. Christian soldiers practice being alert by using their natural senses and listening to the Spirit's promptings to intercede on behalf of what God is doing.

We must understand that we are not just watching our enemy, but also our God. Is God changing somebody's heart? Let us give thanks and pray. Is he stirring a revival? Let us praise and intercede.

What is God doing around you? How is he calling you to intercede?

Prayer in the Spirit Is Persevering

With every prayer and petition, pray at all times in the Spirit, and to this end be alert, with all perseverance and requests for all the saints.
Ephesians 6:18

Paul says that we must pray "with all perseverance." Prayer in the flesh is often short-lived, but Spirit-led prayer is persevering. This is especially important in spiritual warfare, because many of our blessings and victories come only through persevering prayer. Consider what Christ teaches in Luke 11:9-13:

"So I tell you: Ask, and it will be given to you; seek, and you will find; knock, and the door will be opened for you. For everyone who asks receives, and the one who seeks finds, and to the one who knocks, the door will be opened. What father among you, if your son asks for a fish, will give him a snake instead of a fish? Or if he asks for an egg, will give him a scorpion? If you then, although you are evil, know how to give good gifts to your children, how much more will the heavenly Father give the Holy Spirit to those who ask him!"

"Ask, and it will be given to you; seek, and you will find; knock, and the door will be opened for you" (v. 9) can be translated literally, "Ask and keep asking, seek and keep seeking, knock and keep knocking." Christ says there must be perseverance in prayer to receive God's blessing. In addition, consider the promise in verse 13, "How much more will the heavenly Father give the Holy Spirit to those who ask him!" In the Greek, "the" does not precede "Holy Spirit"—it can be translated literally "give Holy Spirit." Many scholars say that when the article is missing, this term does not refer to the person of the Spirit, but rather the ministries of the Spirit.[37]

When you pray with perseverance, God will give you the strength you need, the wisdom and power to conquer habitual sins, and everything else you need to live a godly life. Don't give up! Spirit-led prayer perseveres.

Persevering prayer is also needed because of the spiritual forces we are fighting against. In Daniel 10:10-14, Daniel petitioned God for three weeks and then an angel appeared. The angel said that God had sent him with a response when Daniel first began to pray, but he was caught up in a war with the spiritual forces over Persia. While Daniel continued to pray, the angel Michael came to set the other angel free so he could answer Daniel's request. Yes, persevering prayer is needed because of the spiritual war we are engaged in. We must persevere in prayer for the salvation of a relative, revival in a church or a nation, and any other good work. We must pray at least until God removes the burden of prayer, as he did with Paul when he prayed for healing (2 Cor 12:8-9).

Are you persevering in prayer?

Prayer in the Spirit Is Universal

> With every prayer and petition, pray at all times in the Spirit, and to this end be alert, with all perseverance and requests for all the saints.
> Ephesians 6:18

Prayer in the Spirit is also universal—we pray "for all the saints." I have often been taught to pray specifically and this is correct, but it is also important to pray generally. We are in this war with millions of other Christians we do not know. Does this lack of knowledge mean that we should not pray for them? Absolutely not! We must intercede according to the knowledge we have.

We intercede for the Christians in our church, our nation, and all the nations of the earth. We should remember both persecuted Christians and those living at ease (a temptation in itself). We must especially pray for our spiritual leaders such as missionaries, pastors, and teachers.

I once heard a story about the president of Taylor University in Indiana. While on a flight, he was seated next to a lady who was clearly fasting and praying—every time the food came, she refused it. As he watched her he became very convicted of his own need to pray, so he decided to ask if she was a Christian. However, when asked, the lady responded, "Why no! I am a Satanist, and I'm praying for Christian leaders throughout the world to fall into sin, to turn away from God, and for others to follow them." This is sobering! Certainly, it should encourage us to continually lift up our Christian leaders throughout the world, as they are the target of special attacks by the enemy.

This is a real war, and we are not in it by ourselves. Therefore, we must continually intercede for other believers.
How can we be more faithful in praying for all saints?

1. Keep a prayer list. A list helps us pray faithfully for people we know, and it can also remind us to pray in general for believers in various parts of society and the world.

2. Use a prayer method—like the "Five-Finger Prayer."

Here is a description of it from a Daily Bread devotional:

- "When you fold your hands, the thumb is nearest you. So begin by praying for those closest to you—your loved ones (Philippians 1:3-5).
- The index finger is the pointer. Pray for those who teach—Bible teachers and preachers, and those who teach children (1 Thessalonians 5:25).
- The next finger is the tallest. It reminds you to pray for those in authority over you—national and local leaders, and your supervisor at work (1 Timothy 2:1-2).
- The fourth finger is usually the weakest. Pray for those who are in trouble or who are suffering (James 5:13-16).
- Then comes your little finger. It reminds you of your smallness in relation to God's greatness. Ask Him to supply your needs (Philippians 4:6, 19)."[38]

Prayer in the Spirit is universal—for all saints.

Prayer in the Spirit Is Gospel-Centered and Bible-Centered

> Pray for me also, that I may be given the message when I begin to speak – that I may confidently make known the mystery of the gospel, for which I am an ambassador in chains. Pray that I may be able to speak boldly as I ought to speak.
> Ephesians 6:19-20

Finally, prayer in the Spirit is always consumed with the spread of the gospel and God's Word. While Paul was in prison, he didn't ask the believers to pray for his release. Led by the Spirit, he sought prayer for God to give him the words to preach and the courage to preach them fearlessly. He essentially asked for prayer over the content of the message and the manner it was presented.

Why does Paul mention his need to be fearless in preaching twice in his prayer request?

The fact that he mentions the need for boldness (or to be "fearless") twice shows us his own struggle to preach God's Word faithfully. Such preaching could lead to his death or a longer prison term.

However, this does not just show Paul's great need for boldness in preaching, but also the church's. Most Christians struggle with fear in sharing God's Word. They feel inadequate. They fear the response of people. They fear persecution, for example, in the form of job loss. And therefore most remain quiet. This is also true for preachers. Often there is hesitation to preach the full counsel of God, especially in an age where his Word is widely rejected.

However, like Paul, when we are led by the Spirit, he leads us to pray about the proclamation of the Word (cf. Col 4:3-4, 2 Thess 3:1). We should pray for believers to properly interpret and understand God's Word, and for them to share it in their churches and workplaces, and with their families. In addition, we should pray for the gospel to be received. When this happens, the enemy is defeated as people are translated from darkness to light and set free from strongholds.

The Holy Spirit is the author of the Word of God, as Scripture was inspired by him (cf. 2 Tim 3:16, 2 Peter 1:21). Therefore, he continually encourages people to pray over the Word of God and for it to be shared. Let us continually call on the Holy Spirit to empower his people to share his Word with boldness, for God's kingdom to be built, and for the evil one's kingdom to be destroyed.

Lord, spread your Word throughout the world, bring glory to yourself, and destroy the evil one and all his forces! In Jesus name, we pray.

Conclusion

Before we close, let's consider some words on prayer from John Piper's book, Desiring God:

> Unless I'm badly mistaken, one of the main reasons so many of God's children don't have a significant life of prayer is not so much that we don't want to, but that we don't plan to. If you want to take a four-week vacation, you don't just get up one summer morning and say, "Hey, let's go today!" You won't have anything ready. You won't know where to go. Nothing has been planned.
>
> But that is how many of us treat prayer. We get up day after day and realize that significant times of prayer should be part of our

life, but nothing's ever ready. We don't know where to go. Nothing has been planned. No time. No place. No procedure. And we all know that the opposite of planning is not a wonderful flow of deep, spontaneous experiences in prayer. The opposite of planning is the rut. If you don't plan a vacation you will probably stay home and watch TV! The natural unplanned flow of spiritual life sinks to the lowest ebb of vitality. There is a race to be run and a fight to be fought. If you want renewal in your life of prayer you must plan to see it.

Therefore, my simple exhortation is this: Let us take time this very day to rethink our priorities and how prayer fits in. Make some new resolve. Try some new venture with God. Set a time. Set a place. Choose a portion of Scripture to guide you. Don't be tyrannized by the press of busy days. We all need mid-course corrections. Make this a day of turning to prayer — for the glory of God and for the fullness of your joy.[39]

Reflection

1. How do you aim to pray on all occasions? Are there any insights or disciplines that help you in this endeavor? How is God calling you to grow in constant prayer?
2. What type(s) of prayer are you most prone to pray? How is God calling you to vary your prayers?
3. Are there any answers to prayer that you've received after a long season of praying? If so, what

were they? What are some things that you are still praying for?

4. Do you struggle with boldness when witnessing? Why or why not? How can we overcome our fear of speaking for God? Why is it so important to pray for the preaching of the Word of God?

5. What other questions or thoughts do you have about this section?

6. In what ways can you pray in response? Take time to pray as the Lord leads.

Conclusion

Believers are engaged in spiritual warfare with the enemy of their souls. Satan and his demons are bent on destroying God's works and his people. Our enemy's attacks are varied—he tempts, persecutes, and deceives. How can we stand firm in this spiritual war?

1. Believers stand firm by being prepared (with God's power and character).
2. Believers stand firm by knowing the enemy.
3. Believers stand firm by fighting.
4. Believers stand firm by putting on the belt of truth.
5. Believers stand firm by putting on the breastplate of righteousness.
6. Believers stand firm by putting on the footwear of peace.
7. Believers stand firm by taking up the shield of faith.
8. Believers stand firm by putting on the helmet of salvation.
9. Believers stand firm by taking up the sword of the Spirit.
10. Believers stand firm by praying in the Spirit.

Walking the Romans Road

How can a person be saved? From what is he saved? How can someone have eternal life? Scripture teaches that after death each person will spend eternity either in heaven or hell. How can a person go to heaven?

Paul said this to Timothy:

> You, however, must continue in the things you have learned and are confident about. You know who taught you and how from infancy you have known the holy writings, which are able to give you wisdom for salvation through faith in Christ Jesus.
> 2 Timothy 3:14-15

One of the reasons God gave us Scripture is to make us wise for salvation. This means that without it nobody can know how to be saved.

Well then, how can a people be saved and what are they being saved from? A common method of sharing the good news of salvation is through the Romans Road. One of the great themes, not only of the Bible, but specifically of the book of Romans is salvation. In Romans, the author, Paul, clearly details the steps we must take in order to be saved.

How can we be saved? What steps must we take?

Step One: We Must Accept that We Are Sinners

Romans 3:23 says, "For all have sinned and fall short of the glory of God." What does it mean to sin? The word sin means "to miss the mark." The mark we missed is looking like God. When God created mankind in the Genesis narrative, he created man in the "image of God" (1:27). The "image of God" means many things, but probably, most importantly it means we were made to be holy just as he is holy. Man was made moral. We were meant to reflect God's holiness in every way: the way we think, the way we talk, and the way we act. And any time we miss the mark in these areas, we commit sin.

Furthermore, we do not only sin when we commit a sinful act such as: lying, stealing, or cheating. Again, we sin anytime we have a wrong heart motive. The greatest commandments in Scripture are to "Love the Lord your God with all your heart, with all your soul, and with all your mind" (Matt 22:36-40, paraphrase). Whenever we don't love God supremely and love others as ourselves, we sin and fall short of the glory of God. For this reason, man is always in a state of sinning. Sadly, even if our actions are good, our heart is bad. I have never loved God with my whole heart, mind, and soul and neither has anybody else. Therefore, we have all sinned and fall short of the glory of God (Rom 3:23). We have all missed the mark of God's holiness and we must accept this.

What's the next step?

Step Two: We Must Understand We Are Under the Judgment of God

Why are we under the judgment of God? It is because of our sins. Scripture teaches God is not only a loving God, but he is a just God. And his justice requires judgment for each of our sins. Romans 6:23 says, "For the payoff of sin is death."

A wage is something we earn. Every time we sin, we earn the wage of death. What is death? Death really means separation. In physical death, the body is separated from the spirit, but in spiritual death, man is separated from God. Man currently lives in a state of spiritual death (cf. Eph 2:1-3). We do not love God, obey him, or know him as we should. Therefore, man is in a state of death.

Moreover, one day at our physical death, if we have not been saved, we will spend eternity separated from God in a very real hell. In hell, we will pay the wage for each of our sins. Therefore, in hell people will experience various degrees of punishment (cf. Lk 12:47-48). This places man in a very dangerous predicament—unholy and therefore under the judgment of God.

How should we respond to this? This leads us to our third step.

Step Three: We Must Recognize God Has Invited All to Accept His Free Gift of Salvation

Romans 6:23 does not stop at the wages of sin being death. It says, "For the payoff of sin is death, but the gift of God is eternal life in Christ Jesus our Lord." Because God loved everybody on the earth, he offered the free gift of eternal life, which anyone can receive through Jesus Christ.

Because it is a gift, it cannot be earned. We cannot work for it. Ephesians 2:8-9 says, "For by grace you are saved through faith, and this is not from yourselves, it is the gift of God; it is not from works, so that no one can boast."

Going to church, being baptized, giving to the poor, or doing any other righteous work does not save. Salvation is a gift that must be received from God. It is a gift that has been prepared by his effort alone.

How do we receive this free gift?

Step Four: We Must Believe Jesus Christ Died for Our Sins and Rose from the Dead

If we are going to receive this free gift, we must believe in God's Son, Jesus Christ. Because God loved us, cared for us, and didn't want us to be separated from him eternally, he sent his Son to die for our sins. Romans 5:8 says, "But God demonstrates his own love for us, in that while we were still sinners, Christ died for us." Similarly, John 3:16 says, "For this is the way God loved the world: He gave his one and only Son, so that everyone who believes in him will not perish but have eternal life." God so loved us that he gave his only Son for our sins.

Jesus Christ was a real, historical person who lived 2,000 years ago. He was born of a virgin. He lived a perfect life. He was put to death by the Romans and the Jews. And he rose again on the third day. In his death, he took our sins and God's wrath for them and gave us his perfect righteousness so we could be accepted by God. Second Corinthians 5:21 says, "God made the one who did not know sin to be sin for us, so that in him we would become the righteousness of God." God did all this so we could be saved from his wrath.

Christ's death satisfied the just anger of God over our sins. When God saw Jesus on the cross, he saw us and our sins and therefore judged Jesus. And now, when God sees those who are saved, he sees his righteous Son and accepts us. In salvation, we have become the righteousness of God.

If we are going to be saved, if we are going to receive this free gift of salvation, we must believe in Christ's death, burial, and resurrection for our sins (cf. 1 Cor 15:3-5, Rom 10:9-10). Do you believe?

Step Five: We Must Confess Christ as Lord of Our Lives

Romans 10:9-10 says,

> Because if you confess with your mouth that Jesus is Lord and believe in your heart that God raised him from the dead, you will be saved. For with the heart one believes and thus has righteousness and with the mouth one confesses and thus has salvation.

Not only must we believe, but we must confess Christ as Lord of our lives. It is one thing to believe in Christ but another to follow Christ. Simple belief does not save. Christ must be our Lord. James said this: "...Even the demons believe that – and tremble with fear" (James 2:19), but the demons are not saved—Christ is not their Lord.

Another aspect of making Christ Lord is repentance. Repentance really means a change of mind that leads to a change of direction. Before we met Christ, we were living our own life and following our own sinful desires. But when we get saved, our mind and direction change. We start to follow Christ as Lord.

How do we make this commitment to the lordship of Christ so we can be saved? Paul said we must confess with our mouth "Jesus is Lord" as we believe in him. Romans 10:13 says, "For everyone who calls on the name of the Lord will be saved."

If you admit that you are a sinner and understand you are under God's wrath because of them; if you believe Jesus Christ is the Son of God, that he died on the cross for your sins, and rose from the dead for your salvation; if you are ready to turn from your sin and cling to Christ as Lord, you can be saved.

If this is your heart, then you can pray this prayer and commit to following Christ as your Lord.

> *Dear heavenly Father, I confess I am a sinner and have fallen short of your glory, what you made me for. I believe Jesus Christ died on the cross to pay the penalty for my sins and rose from the dead so I can have eternal life. I am turning away from my sin and accepting you as my Lord and Savior. Come into my life and change me. Thank you for your gift of salvation.*

Scripture teaches that if you truly accepted Christ as your Lord, then you are a new creation. Second Corinthians 5:17 says, "So then, if anyone is in Christ, he is a new creation; what is old has passed away – look, what is new has come!" God has forgiven your sins (1 John 1:9), he has given you his Holy Spirit (Rom 8:15), and he is going to disciple you and make you into the image of his Son (cf. Rom 8:29). He will never leave you nor forsake you (Heb 13:5), and he will complete the work he has begun in your life (Phil 1:6). In heaven, angels and saints are rejoicing because of your commitment to Christ (Lk 15:7).

Praise God for his great salvation! May God keep you in his hand, empower you through the Holy Spirit, train you through mature believers, and use you to build his kingdom! "He who calls you is trustworthy, and he will in fact do this" (1 Thess 5:24). God bless you!

Coming Soon

Praise the Lord for your interest in studying and teaching God's Word. If God has blessed you through the BTG series, please partner with us in petitioning God to greatly use this series to encourage and build his Church. Also, please consider leaving an Amazon review and signing up for free book promotions. By doing this, you help spread the "Word." Thanks for your partnership in the gospel from the first day until now (Phil 1:4-5).

Available:
First Peter
Theology Proper
Building Foundations for a Godly Marriage
Colossians
God's Battle Plan for Purity
Nehemiah
Philippians
The Perfections of God
The Armor of God
Ephesians
Abraham
Finding a Godly Mate
1 Timothy
The Beatitudes
Equipping Small Group Leaders
2 Timothy
Jacob

Coming Soon:
The Sermon on the Mount

About the Author

Greg Brown earned his MA in religion and MA in teaching from Trinity International University, a MRE from Liberty University, and a PhD in theology from Louisiana Baptist University. He has served over fourteen years in pastoral ministry, and currently serves as chaplain and professor at Handong Global University, teaching pastor at Handong International Congregation, and as a Navy Reserve chaplain.

Greg married his lovely wife, Tara Jayne, in 2006, and they have one daughter, Saiyah Grace. He enjoys going on dates with his wife, playing with his daughter, reading, writing, studying in coffee shops, working out, and following the NBA and UFC. His pursuit in life, simply stated, is "to know God and to be found faithful by Him."

To connect with Greg, please follow at http://www.pgregbrown.com.

Notes

[1] MacArthur, J. F., Jr. (1986). *Ephesians* (pp. 337–338). Chicago: Moody Press.

[2] MacArthur, J. F., Jr. (1986). *Ephesians* (p. 344). Chicago: Moody Press.

[3] Stott, J. R. W. (1979). *God's new society: the message of Ephesians* (pp. 266–267). Downers Grove, IL: InterVarsity Press.

[4] Foulkes, F. (1989). *Ephesians: an introduction and commentary* (Vol. 10, p. 175). Downers Grove, IL: InterVarsity Press.

[5] MacArthur, J. F., Jr. (1986). *Ephesians* (p. 338). Chicago: Moody Press.

[6] Accessed 10/31/2015 from http://global.britannica.com/topic/legion

[7] Wiersbe, W. W. (1996). *The Bible exposition commentary* (Vol. 2, p. 57). Wheaton, IL: Victor Books.

[8] Stott, J. R. W. (1979). *God's new society: the message of Ephesians* (p. 264). Downers Grove, IL: InterVarsity Press.

[9] MacDonald, W. (1995). *Believer's Bible Commentary: Old and New Testaments*. (A. Farstad, Ed.) (p. 1952). Nashville: Thomas Nelson.

[10] Hughes, R. K. (1990). *Ephesians: the mystery of the body of Christ* (p. 215). Wheaton, IL: Crossway Books.

[11] MacArthur, J. F., Jr. (1986). *Ephesians* (p. 341). Chicago: Moody Press.

[12] MacArthur, J. F., Jr. (1986). *Ephesians* (p. 340). Chicago: Moody Press.

[13] MacDonald, W. (1995). *Believer's Bible Commentary: Old and New Testaments*. (A. Farstad, Ed.) (p. 1952). Nashville: Thomas Nelson.

[14] Boice, J. M. (1988). *Ephesians: an expositional commentary* (pp. 244–245). Grand Rapids, MI: Ministry Resources Library.

[15] Accessed 11/14/2015 from https://en.wikipedia.org/wiki/Peter_Singer#Bestiality

[16] Accessed 11/14/2015 from https://bible.org/seriespage/lesson-57-protected-truth-and-righteousness-ephesians-614

[17] Hughes, R. K. (1990). *Ephesians: the mystery of the body of Christ* (p. 224). Wheaton, IL: Crossway Books.

[18] Wiersbe, W. W. (1996). *The Bible exposition commentary* (Vol. 2, p. 58). Wheaton, IL: Victor Books.

[19] Foulkes, F. (1989). *Ephesians: an introduction and commentary* (Vol. 10, p. 179). Downers Grove, IL: InterVarsity Press.

[20] MacArthur, J. F., Jr. (1986). *Ephesians* (pp. 350–351). Chicago: Moody Press.

[21] MacArthur, J. F., Jr. (1986). *Ephesians* (p. 351). Chicago: Moody Press.

[22] MacArthur, J. F., Jr. (1986). *Ephesians* (p. 351). Chicago: Moody Press.

[23] MacArthur, J. F., Jr. (1986). *Ephesians* (p. 354). Chicago: Moody Press.

[24] MacArthur, J. F., Jr. (1986). *Ephesians* (pp. 358–359). Chicago: Moody Press.

[25] MacArthur, J. F., Jr. (1986). *Ephesians* (pp. 358–359). Chicago: Moody Press.

[26] Wiersbe, W. W. (1996). *The Bible exposition commentary* (Vol. 2, p. 58). Wheaton, IL: Victor Books.

[27] Boice, J. M. (1988). *Ephesians: an expositional commentary* (p. 248). Grand Rapids, MI: Ministry Resources Library.

[28] MacArthur, J. F., Jr. (1986). *Ephesians* (pp. 367–368). Chicago: Moody Press.

[29] MacArthur, J. F., Jr. (1986). *Ephesians* (p. 370). Chicago: Moody Press.

[30] Boice, J. M. (1988). *Ephesians: an expositional commentary* (p. 252). Grand Rapids, MI: Ministry Resources Library.

[31] Accessed 11/23/2015 from http://www.biblestudytools.com/lexicons/hebrew/nas/hagah.html

[32] Accessed 11/23/2015 from http://www.mljtrust.org/sermons/

[33] Hughes, R. K. (1990). *Ephesians: the mystery of the body of Christ* (pp. 247–250). Wheaton, IL: Crossway Books.

[34] Accessed 11/28/2015 from https://bible.org/seriespage/lesson-62-how-fight-god-ephesians-618-20

[35] Hughes, R. K. (1990). *Ephesians: the mystery of the body of Christ* (p. 251). Wheaton, IL: Crossway Books.

[36] MacArthur, J. F., Jr. (1986). *Ephesians* (p. 380). Chicago: Moody Press.

[37] MacDonald, W. (1995). *Believer's Bible Commentary: Old and New Testaments*. (A. Farstad, Ed.) (p. 1413). Nashville: Thomas Nelson.
[38] Accessed 11/28/2015 from http://odb.org/2005/06/02/five-finger-prayers/
[39] John Piper, *Desiring God* (Portland, OR: Multnomah, 1986), pp. 150, 151.

Made in the USA
Columbia, SC
14 October 2020